Mary Lincoln's
DRESSMAKER

Mary Lincoln's DRESSMAKER

ELIZABETH KECKLEY'S
REMARKABLE RISE
FROM SLAVE TO
WHITE HOUSE
CONFIDANTE

BECKY RUTBERG

WALKER AND COMPANY
NEW YORK

Elizabeth Keckley's autobiography, Behind the Scenes or Thirty Years a Slave and Four Years in the White House, *was first published by Carleton & Company in New York in 1868. Quotes in this biography, appearing as dialogue, come from Mrs. Keckley's book.*

First published in the United States of America in 1995 by Walker Publishing Company, Inc.

Published simultaneously in Canada by Thomas Allen & Son Canada, Limited, Markham, Ontario

Library of Congress Cataloging-in-Publication Data
Rutberg, Becky.
Mary Lincoln's dressmaker : Elizabeth Keckley's remarkable rise from slave to White House confidante / Becky Rutberg.
p.   cm.
Includes bibliographical references and index.
ISBN 0-8027-8224-8 (hardcover). — ISBN 0-8027-8225-6 (reinforced)
1. Keckley, Elizabeth, 1818–1907—Juvenile literature.
2. Lincoln, Mary Todd, 1818–1882—Employees—Biography—Juvenile literature.   3. Slaves—United States—Biography—Juvenile literature.   4. Dressmakers—United States—Biography—Juvenile literature.   I. Title.
E457.2.K39R87   1995
973.7'092—dc20
[B]   94-45839
CIP
AC

Frontispiece daguerreotype by Nicholas H. Shepherd appears courtesy of the Lincoln Museum, Fort Wayne, Indiana, a part of the Lincoln National Corporation.

Book design by Claire Naylon Vaccaro

Printed in the United States of America

2   4   6   8   10   9   7   5   3   1

To those former slaves
whose stories died with them.

ACKNOWLEDGMENTS

Without love and support, my dreams of writing *Mary Lincoln's Dressmaker* would not have been realized. First, I want to thank my husband, David, and our children, Samara, Raquel, Bryan, and Morgan, who listened patiently for more than ten years to my ramblings, self-doubts, and misgivings while I wrote Lizzie Keckley's story. They never lost faith that someday I'd "get it together."

My sincere gratitude to Don Freeman of the *San Diego Union-Tribune*, whose encouragement convinced me that I could write professionally if I wanted to badly enough and persisted. Heartfelt thanks to children's author Laurence Pringle, who rekindled my spirit when it failed. And to my Wednesday-morning critique group, who heard the same chapters over and over for more than five years and offered priceless criticism, encouragement, and advice: Deanne Durrett, Robin Rierdan, Virginia Russell, Glenda Palmer, Susan Wilson, Florence Atchinson, Sue Bodow, Maggie Hayko, Jan Callis, Connie Plantz, and Virginia Aldape (whose courage, fortitude, and wisdom often raised my flagging spirit). A special tribute to Dr. Craig A. Brown. Thank you to Estelle Raefsky Alexander, my longtime friend, for her professional assistance as a librarian and to her sister, Alice Raefsky, whose life inspired mine. To my friend Marianne Raphaely, and her mother, Teresa M. Carrano, whose belief in my endeavor never wavered. And to Jimmy Olgers of Dinwiddie Courthouse, Virginia, for his gracious hospitality and delicious watermelon during my research travels.

Sincere thanks also to Abby Gilbert, past president of the United States Treasury Historical Association, who gave unstintingly of her time to search through the Treasury Archives for information. And to Dr. Frances Diamond, my right hand at the end of this project. No acknowledgment would be complete without special mention of the private and public institutions whose collections and staff provided information and photographs: the Missouri Historical Society at St. Louis, especially Carol S. Verble, assistant librarian, and Kirsten Hammerstrom, curatorial assistant in Photographs and Prints; the State Historical Society of Missouri at Columbus; the Mercantile Library of St. Louis; the St. Louis Genealogical Society, especially Herman Radloff; the Eggleston Library of Hampden-Sydney College, especially Catherine Pollari, librarian; Moorland-Spingarn Library of Howard University, especially Donna Wells of the Prints and Photographs Division; the Schomburg Center for Research in Black Culture of the New York Public Library; the R. E. Stokes Learning Resource Center Library of Wilberforce University, especially Jacqueline Brown, reference librarian; the Vicksburg and Warren County Historical Society, especially Mrs. Blanche Terry; the Illinois State Historical Society; the Chicago Historical Society; Terry Fife and Leslie Schuster, at the company History Works, in Oak Park, Illinois; the Historic Hillsborough Commission, especially Josephine H. Barbour; the Washington Historical Society; the Baltimore County Historical Society; the Virginia Historical Society, especially Francis Pollard, reference librarian; the Minnesota Historical Society; the Probate Division of St. Louis Circuit Court and the Probate Division of Washington, D.C.; the Library of Congress, in particular its Rare Manuscript Division; the University of California at San Diego; and the Latter-Day Saints Family History Library of San Diego.

To the above people and institutions, I shall be forever indebted.

Mary Lincoln's
DRESSMAKER

CHAPTER ONE

ELIZABETH HOBBS KECKLEY worked her way around crowds of congressmen, reporters, office seekers, and visitors who packed the lobby and the halls of Willard's Hotel to catch a glimpse of President-elect Abraham Lincoln on his way to the Capitol for Inauguration Day ceremonies.

Lizzie had spent the first thirty-seven years of her life as a slave. Now a successful dressmaker, she hoped to enlist the new president's wife, Mary Todd Lincoln, as one of her clients.

Elizabeth Hobbs Keckley, frontispiece in Behind the Scenes, *1868.* (USED BY PERMISSION OF THE MISSOURI HISTORICAL SOCIETY.)

Lizzie's dressmaking client Mrs. John McClean had met her at the entrance to the hotel and directed her to Parlor 6 on the second floor, where the Lincolns were lodging until their move to the White House. Mrs. McClean had promised to recommend her to Mrs. Lincoln as a mantuamaker—a highly skilled dressmaker—in exchange for a ball gown that

Crowds watching President Lincoln take his first inaugural oath of office March 4, 1861, in front of the unfinished dome of the Capitol. (COURTESY OF THE LIBRARY OF CONGRESS.)

Lizzie created and assembled on very short notice. At the time, Lizzie had more orders for ball gowns, traveling costumes, riding clothes, and visiting ensembles than she could possibly complete. But an introduction and recommendation to the president's wife was too good to be true.

Lizzie later recalled the first time she met Mrs. Lincoln. "With a nervous step, I passed on, and knocked at Mrs. Lincoln's door. A cheery voice bade me come in and a lady, inclined to stoutness, about forty years of age, stood before me."

Mrs. Lincoln said, "You are Lizzie Keckley, I believe, the dressmaker Mrs. McClean recommended. . . . I have not the time to talk to you now, but would like you to call at the White House at 8 o'clock tomorrow morning where I shall then be."

Lizzie had been speechless. She'd bowed, left the room, returned to the Walker Lewis Boardinghouse five blocks away.

Outside the building hundreds of people waiting to witness the inaugural ceremonies slept on market stalls and piles of lumber stacked along Pennsylvania Avenue. Not a bed or single indoor space for lodging could be had. Some people walked the streets all night. Dust from scraping Pennsylvania Avenue the night before in preparation for the inaugural parade covered everything and everyone. Public fountains served as washing troughs for shivering visitors without accommodations.

Fear pervaded the city. The country was on the brink of civil war. President-elect Lincoln told men to keep their wives at home because he expected bullets to be flying that day. Rumors circulated that Virginia horsemen intended to kidnap Mr. Lincoln.

Militiamen poised with rifles stood on rooftops ready for trouble along the inaugural parade route. Cannons ready to fire at a moment's notice blockaded side streets. Wooden shutters on houses were tightly closed.

The Capitol Building's unfinished dome was surrounded with scaffolding under which President-elect Lincoln would be sworn into office and deliver his inau-

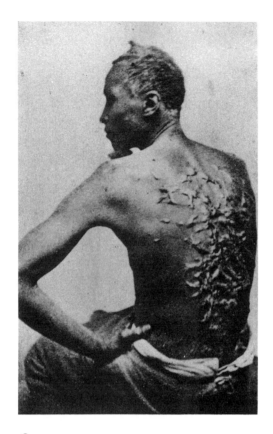

Scars from brutal whippings (1863). (COURTESY OF
THE MASSACHUSETTS COMMANDERY MILITARY ORDER OF
THE LOYAL LEGION AND THE U.S. ARMY MILITARY
HISTORY INSTITUTE.)

gural address. It seemed to represent the unfinished business of the nation.

After what seemed like an endless night, Lizzie crossed
the threshold of the White House the next morning at

8:00 A.M. Armed and uniformed sentries stood posted at surrounding iron gates and guarded outer doors. Thin, short, jovial Edward McManus, the official White House doorkeeper, checked names from a list of expected visitors.

Lizzie was shown upstairs to a large public waiting room furnished with ornate mahogany furniture.

Lizzie's hope all but vanished when she discovered three well-known mantuamakers also waiting for an appointment with Mrs. Lincoln. It appeared the first lady had asked several women to recommend the specialized dressmakers.

Lizzie felt defeated. How could she, a former slave who carried whiplash scars on her back, compete with free white women?

CHAPTER TWO

LIZZIE KECKLEY'S FIRST duty as a slave was to attend to her mistress's newborn daughter. Mrs. Mary Cole Burwell promised that if four-year-old Lizzie watched carefully over the infant, rocked her cradle, kept flies away from her face, and prevented her from crying, she would be the baby's maid. Lizzie wanted nothing more. The job meant that she could work in the "big house" near her mother, the Burwells' Agnes. Agnes sewed for the eleven members of the Burwell family and for the seventy slaves they owned at one time or another. Agnes and Lizzie lived in a rough-hewn one-room cabin that let in cold and rain as well as light and made sleep impossible, especially during the summer months.

On the day of her first assignment, in 1822, Lizzie wore a short, coarse tunic covered by a small white apron. When she saw the newborn child, she looked upon her as a little pet and began rocking the cradle playfully and enthusiastically. Suddenly the child flipped from the cradle onto the floor.

Not knowing what to do, and fearful of touching the baby, Lizzie grabbed the fireplace shovel and tried to shovel her charge back into the cradle. Mrs. Burwell heard the commotion from the next room and ordered Lizzie from the house, demanding that she be whipped for her carelessness.

The whipping post stood near the barn and the

smokehouse at the far end of the Hampden-Sydney College campus located in the heart of Virginia's Edward County where Lizzie's master, Colonel Armistead Burwell, worked as steward.

Lizzie described her first beating in the book she wrote many years later: "The blows were not administered with a light hand . . . and . . . the severity of the lashing has made me remember the incident . . . well."

The colonel's salary depended on the number of students enrolled at the all-male Presbyterian college. Each student paid him a fee to deliver wood and water to bedrooms, prepare and serve meals, fix broken windows, clean and repair classrooms, and maintain the buildings on the campus. The colonel's slaves fulfilled his duties for him.

After his first year on the job in 1822, student enrollment dropped, so the colonel sold slaves to compensate for his loss of income. In 1825 when he did not have enough money to pay the hog farmer for that winter's supply of pork, he ordered his cook, Martha, to dress her young son, Little Joe, in his Sunday best and send him to the smokehouse.

Lizzie recalled the incident and the heartache vividly. She wrote that Little Joe "came in [to the smokehouse] with a bright face, was placed in the scales, and was sold, like the hogs, at so much per pound."

When Little Joe was seated in a wagon next to the hog farmer, his mother pleaded with the colonel not to take her boy from her. The colonel told her the boy was simply going to the nearby town of Petersburg and would return in the morning.

Morning after morning passed, and the child never returned.

When Little Joe's mother wept day after day over her lost son, the colonel had her whipped. He and his wife insisted that their slaves look pleasant no matter how they felt.

The incident moved Lizzie to observe, "The sunny face of the slave is not always an indication of sunshine in the heart."

Enrollment at Hampden-Sydney College continued to drop, and the colonel sold more and more of his slaves, often separating children from mothers and wives from husbands. Lizzie's mother was forced to perform more and more chores. Fearful for her mother's health, eight-year-old Lizzie learned to knit, sew, and work at other tasks to ease her mother's burden. Some of these chores required so much strength that she later com-

Hampden-Sydney College, circa 1830. Slave cabins stood outside the gates of the college campus. The steward's house, where Colonel Burwell lived, is at the extreme left. The kitchen is in the rear. The college building is in the center, with the library directly beside it. The president's house is at the extreme right. (COURTESY OF DOUGLAS PAYNE, COPYRIGHT © HAMPDEN-SYDNEY COLLEGE.)

mented that "her young energies were taxed to their fullest."

No matter how hard she worked, however, Lizzie's mistress told her repeatedly that she was not worth the money it cost to keep her. These words echoed over and over in Lizzie's mind for years. She often wondered why words so thoughtlessly and carelessly spoken, especially when spoken by a woman so difficult to please, could hurt so much.

Throughout Lizzie's life she would constantly strive to prove herself, often overtaxing her strength and sacrificing her own welfare for that of others.

· · ·

Reverend Robert A. Burwell, 1802–95, Lizzie's owner in North Carolina. (COURTESY OF THE HISTORIC HILLSBOROUGH COMMISSION, NORTH CAROLINA.)

George Pleasant Hobbs, the man Lizzie knew as her father, was the slave of another master who lived in the town of Dinwiddie Courthouse, Virginia, almost 100 miles away. George's master permitted him to visit his family twice a year, at Christmas and Easter. During those visits he would proudly hold Lizzie at arm's length and fondly call her "little Lizzie." Lizzie remembered his saying to his wife, "She is growing into a large fine girl. I dun no which I like best, you or Lizzie, as both are so dear to me."

One Christmas, in an unusual gesture of kindness, the colonel offered to buy George Hobbs from his master.

Lizzie remembered her mother's joy. "It was a bright day for my mother when it was announced that my father was coming to live with us. The old weary look faded from her face, and she worked as if her heart was in every task."

That Christmas, however, while her parents spoke hopefully of the future, the colonel came to their crude cabin, holding a letter from George's master. The colonel informed them that plans had changed. He did not have money to buy George, and worse still, George's master had ordered his immediate return. He planned to move to Tennessee and take George with him.

The announcement struck the family like a thunderbolt. Lizzie never forgot her father's last moments with them—his last kiss, his frantic clutching of her mother to his breast, his prayers, the tears and sobs—the anguish of broken hearts. One last good-bye, and her father was gone forever.

Anna Burwell, 1810–71, Lizzie's second mistress. (COURTESY OF THE HISTORIC HILLSBOROUGH COMMISSION, NORTH CAROLINA.)

Agnes's grief over the loss of her husband angered her mistress. One day Mrs. Burwell sputtered, "Stop your nonsense. There is no necessity for you putting on airs. Your husband is not the only one who has had to ´ art. There are plenty more men about here, and if you want a husband so badly, stop crying and go find another."

Agnes stopped grieving outwardly, but Lizzie noted that the light in her eyes had died.

Lizzie's parents had taught themselves the rudiments of reading and writing, and now they wrote to each other regularly. Lizzie treasured her father's letters to Agnes, which were filled with love and hope that the future would bring them together. In nearly every letter there was a message for Lizzie. "Tell my darling little Lizzie to be a good girl, and learn her book. Kiss her for me, and tell her that I will come to see her some day."

Although the family lived in hope, Lizzie and her mother never saw George Hobbs again.

In 1830, so few students enrolled at Hampden-Sydney that the colonel left his job, sold most of his slaves, and moved to Dinwiddie Courthouse, taking Lizzie and her mother with him.

The following year, when Lizzie was almost fourteen, the colonel sent her to live with his eldest son, Robert, and Robert's new wife, Anna, in Chesterfield County, just across the Appomattox River from Dinwiddie. Robert Burwell, a minister, had been a student at Hampden-Sydney College when Lizzie lived there, and she remembered him as a kind and considerate young man. But who knew what slavery would bring out in him as an adult? Slavery had a way of bringing out the worst in both master and slave.

Robert's wife brought no slaves of her own to the marriage, and because she and her husband lived on the reverend's small income, they were too poor to buy a slave of their own. So the colonel lent Lizzie to them.

Lizzie's relationship with her new mistress—whom she addressed as Miss Anna—was poor from the very beginning. Lizzie performed the work of three servants, yet Miss Anna scolded her repeatedly and rarely let her out of her sight, certainly not long enough to cross the river to visit with her mother.

Lizzie attributed Miss Anna's harshness to the reverend's meager salary and her embarrassment at bringing no slaves to the marriage.

Outside influences, however, were also at work. In 1831, the year Lizzie came to live with the reverend and his wife, a slave rebellion occurred. It shattered slaveowners' general belief that slaves were either happy with their lot or too fearful to rebel.

In the Virginia county of Hampton, the slave Nat Turner voluntarily returned to slavery after successfully escaping to the North. He came back to free all slaves and punish their masters. First he killed his own master and the master's family, then encouraged other slaves to join him and kill their oppressors. Authorities crushed the rebellion, and several slaves were hanged, including Nat Turner.

Nevertheless, slaveholders were fearful of more slave uprisings. They slept behind locked doors with loaded guns under their pillows. Some demanded that slaves first taste their food to ensure it wasn't poisoned. They pressured Southern state legislatures to strengthen the Black Codes, restrictive laws that governed every aspect of a slave's life. These legislatures now passed stricter laws with the following provisions: Severe penalties were imposed for teaching slaves to read and write; slaves were forbidden to own property, buy or sell goods, or assemble in groups of more than five; and slaves were not permitted to defend themselves against white people's aggression, to own or carry a weapon, or to testify in court against a white person.

In angry response to the stricter Black Codes, many people in Northern states called for an end to slavery and formed abolitionist societies. They invited runaway slaves to meetings to tell firsthand of the brutal acts committed against them and other blacks. The first abolitionist newspaper, the *Liberator*, founded that year by William Lloyd Garrison, published vehement antislavery articles. Distributed throughout the North, the paper found its way into the hands of many Southern slaveowners. Fearful slaveowners tightened their control over slaves and punished them even more severely for minor offenses.

The years passed slowly. Despite repeated attempts to crush her spirit, Lizzie grew strong and healthy and strikingly beautiful. At seventeen, she was tall and lean with light coffee-colored skin. Long black lashes swept her large gray eyes, which glimmered with intelligence and sparkled with defiance. She moved with an agility and grace that failed to be hidden by the shapeless tunics she wore.

An unspoken rule in slavery forbade slaves to dress in finery, even old finery. Mistresses could be viciously jealous of a young beautiful slave. It was not uncommon for masters to have sex with attractive slaves. When the women became pregnant, masters rarely took responsibility for the slave or the child. Wives often insisted that any children born from their husband's slave relationship be sold.

When Lizzie was eighteen, Reverend Robert moved to a new parish in Hillsborough, North Carolina. Lizzie wondered if she would ever see her mother again.

To supplement her husband's meager income, Miss Anna began teaching girls in her home. The small school soon developed into a boarding school where thirty-eight girls from neighboring states and counties came to live and learn. Courses in history, literature, chemistry, algebra, music, and painting were taught in individual classrooms in freestanding buildings erected near the "big house." The southeast bedroom of the main house served as a dormitory for six girls; other students lived with families in the neighboring town.

Lizzie was surrounded by educational opportunities, yet they were all forbidden to her. She observed the young white women improving themselves each day through learning. They looked forward to a good life, while she faced one of unending servitude. Lizzie grew more sullen, resentful, and spiteful. And her mistress grew more furious.

Lizzie's behavior must have been a source of embarrassment to Miss Anna, who believed discipline built character and whose students came from slaveholding families who expected slaves to be subservient. She became more determined than ever to "put Lizzie in her place." First she pleaded with her husband to whip Lizzie, but he refused. Then she persuaded Mr. Bingham, a neighbor and frequent visitor to the parish, to discipline her.

Bingham occasionally hired Lizzie's time for babysitting services. At his home one Saturday evening while Lizzie bent over a cradle, having just put a baby to sleep, Bingham ordered her to follow him to his study. He closed the door and demanded she bare her back for a flogging. Astounded and indignant, Lizzie demanded to know the reason. When he answered that he was not compelled to give her one, Lizzie promptly retorted, "You shall not whip me unless you prove the stronger.

Nobody has a right to whip me but my own master, and nobody shall do so if I can prevent it."

After a bitter struggle, he bound her hands and tore the dress from her back.

Lizzie described the whipping in her book: "He picked up a rawhide and began to ply it freely over my shoulders . . . with fearful force the rawhide descended. . . . It cut the skin, raised great welts, and the warm blood trickled down my back. Oh God! I can feel the torture now—the terrible, excruciating agony of those moments."

Lizzie refused to let Bingham know how much she suffered. "I closed my lips firmly, that not even a groan might escape from them, and I stood like a statue while the keen lash cut deep into my flesh."

As soon as Lizzie was released, bruised and bleeding and stunned with pain, she ran to the Burwells' home and burst into their parlor, where the reverend and Miss Anna were reading. She demanded an explanation. When the reverend waved her away and told her not to bother him, Lizzie refused to leave and insisted on an answer. He seized the nearest chair and struck her across her raw back. When it came to his slave, he was not the nice man Lizzie remembered from Hampden-Sydney College, but cruel and inhuman.

Falling under the heavy blow, engulfed in pain, Lizzie crept from the room. She dressed her bruises the best she could, but sleep was impossible.

"No, I could not sleep," she wrote, "for I was suffering mental as well as physical torture. My spirit rebelled against the unjustice that had been inflicted upon me, and though I tried to smother my anger and to forgive those who had been so cruel to me, it was impossible."

The next morning, however, she felt somewhat better and was ready to forgive everyone their cruelty for just one kind word. But none came. Lizzie acknowledged to herself that she had provoked Miss Anna's anger, but she also knew her behavior would become worse with Miss Anna's unrelenting drive to crush her.

The next week, Bingham ordered her to his study, prepared with a new rope and whip. Another brutal attack occurred. Lizzie bit his finger so hard, he blindly grabbed a nearby cane and beat her shamelessly. Lizzie summoned all her inner strength, stood tall, clenched her teeth, and refused to utter a sound of pain.

The following Thursday the third beating took place. Lizzie bit her lip until it bled, but uttered no sound. On this occasion, however, Bingham burst into tears. Between sobs, he muttered that it would be a sin before the Almighty Himself to beat her any more. He asked her forgiveness and was never known to whip another servant.

More angry and frustrated than ever, Miss Anna finally persuaded her husband to discipline Lizzie. One day he grabbed the handle of an oak broom and struck Lizzie repeatedly. She fought with all her strength but once again failed to stop the blows. Even so, she kept her silence. Miss Anna witnessed each beating. The third time she was moved by the sight of Lizzie's bleeding body. She fell to her knees and begged her husband to stop. As Lizzie noted, "My distress even touched her cold, jealous heart."

Lizzie was so badly bruised, she was unable to leave her bed for five days.

On April 10, 1838, she wrote about her despair in a letter to her mother:

> I could fill 10 pages with my griefs and misfortunes . . . no tongue could express them as I feel . . . don't forget me tho and answer my letter soon. . . . I will write you again, and would write more now, but Miss Anna says it is time I had finished. Tell Miss Elizabeth [the baby Lizzie had rocked out of her cradle sixteen years before] that I wish she would make haste and get married, for mistress says that I belong to her when she gets married.
>
> Farewell darling mother,
Your affectionate daughter,
Elizabeth Hobbs

Although it seemed that Lizzie had overcome her oppressors, they found other ways to crush her spirit. They permitted and probably encouraged Alexander Kirkland, a wealthy plantation owner who lived down the road, to have sex with Lizzie against her will. This went on for over four years. To her utter dismay, Lizzie became pregnant with this man's child when she was twenty-two years old.

Lizzie wrote of her pain: "The savage efforts to subdue my pride were not the only things that brought me suffering and deep mortification during my residence at Hillsboro. I was regarded as fair-looking for one of my race, and for four years a white man—I spare the world his name—had base designs on me. I do not care to dwell on this subject, for it is one fraught with pain. . . . I became a mother."

CHAPTER THREE

IN 1839 OR 1840, soon after the birth of Lizzie's son, whom she named George after George Pleasant Hobbs, the man she loved as her father, she and the baby were sent from Hillsborough to the reverend's younger sister, Ann Garland. Ann, who was pregnant with her fourth child, Fannie, also operated a school for girls. She, her husband, Hugh, and their three children—Hugh Jr., Mary, and Carrie—lived in Dinwiddie Courthouse, Virginia, in a large eighteenth-century house called Mansfield. It stood on the banks of the Appomattox River only a few miles from where the elder Burwells rented property, where Lizzie's mother lived.

Although still forbidden to partake of any educational opportunities, Lizzie spent four peaceful years at Mansfield, marred only by the fact that her son couldn't live there. Colonel Burwell had ordered that the infant be sent to him to be cared for by Lizzie's mother. An attractive young black man, James Keckley, worked nearby and came to call on her. She discouraged his attentions because she didn't want their relationship to become serious. Lizzie's wounds from the Robert Burwells' abuse healed and she grew close to the Garlands' young growing family.

In 1844 when Colonel Burwell died and old Mrs. Burwell moved in with one of her daughters, Lizzie's mother and four-year-old George joined Lizzie.

Lizzie's delight in having her small family united was short-lived. Within months the Garlands lost all their savings through worthless real estate investments and cosigning loans for friends who failed to repay them.

Four years earlier, Garland had left a successful city law practice in order to move to Mansfield, where he spent his time writing a biography of John Randolph, one of the signers of the Declaration of Independence. Now forced to abandon his writing, Garland left his family to build a new law practice in St. Louis, Missouri, a growing city on the banks of the Mississippi River. He promised to send for them as soon as he was established.

Several months later he sent for his family. Lizzie was shocked when she first saw Garland. He looked worn and old. The house he had rented contained little furniture, and there was no money for anything other than bare necessities.

Soon after their arrival, Garland summoned Lizzie's mother to his study and informed her that he intended to hire her out to other families because they needed the money she could make as a dressmaker.

Lizzie was horrified by this prospect. She later wrote, "The idea was shocking. . . . I could not bear the thought of her going to work for strangers. She had been raised in the family and had watched the growth of each child from infancy. They had received her kindest care. My mother, my poor aged mother, go among strangers to toil for a living! No! . . . I would rather work my fingers to the bone, bend over my sewing 'til the film of blindness gathered in my eyes, nay even beg from street to street."

Lizzie threw herself at Garland's feet. She begged

him to hire her out in place of her mother. Reluctantly he agreed on the condition that she earn enough to support his family.

Slowly, orders began coming in as Lizzie's fashions attracted favorable notice. Women in this era were not supposed to show their knowledge and intelligence. They were expected to be charming and pretty, and confine their talk to light subject matter. So clothing became a way for women to try to show more of their personality than polite conversation permitted. Women either made their own clothes or hired a professional dressmaker. The only store-bought dresses available in 1845 were sacklike, one-size-fits-all models in inexpensive calico or gingham.

St. Louis women who hired dressmakers required a variety of winter outfits for dinner parties, receptions, balls, and ice-skating festivals. During the summer months they needed gowns for the theater and ensembles for different sporting events, fairs, picnics, and swimming.

Although the Garlands were poor, they were invited to the finest festivities hosted by the social elite of the city. Lizzie's dressmaking clientele took much of her time, and when there were many costumes to measure, cut, and sew, she often spent several nights at a patron's home. She made sure, however, that the Garlands dressed well, and she took special pride in dressing their two teenage daughters, Mary and Carrie.

When Mrs. Garland gave birth to her fourth daughter and fifth child, Nannie, the baby became Lizzie's special charge. When the child learned to walk, she followed Lizzie about and insisted on sleeping in Lizzie's bed. Mrs.

Last sale of slaves on the St. Louis Courthouse steps. Oil on canvas by Thomas Satterwhite Noble. (BY PERMISSION OF THE MISSOURI HISTORICAL SOCIETY.)

Garland gave birth to two more children: another daughter, Maggie, and a son, Spottswood.

At this time James Keckley, the man who had courted Lizzie in Virginia, came to St. Louis and asked her to marry him. Lizzie refused, although she liked him more than just as a friend.

She later explained why she had turned him down: "I could not bear the thought of bringing children into slavery—of adding one single recruit to the millions bound to hopeless servitude, fettered and shackled with chains stronger and heavier than manacles of iron."

Young George's birth had been bad enough. How long would it be before the Garlands' son, Hugh Jr., just four years older than her boy, would order him about as his slave? Young George's skin was as white as Hugh's, yet he was a slave.

St. Louis functioned as a slave-trading center while Lizzie lived there. Thirty-two slave dealers operated businesses in the city, collecting slaves from other places and selling them to work on plantations of the Deep South, where they were sometimes worked to death.

On her travels about St. Louis, Lizzie often saw columns of slaves shuffling along, tightly linked by handcuffs and chains looped through iron collars soldered around their necks. They were driven through the streets under the crack of a slave driver's whip, like so many horses and cows, to Bernard M. Lynch's "nigger pen," which stood across from the county courthouse near the wharf. There, in an enclosed dirt yard, barefoot men and women, scantily clad in tunics of osnaburg, or "nigger cloth," milled about as they waited, fearfully, to be auctioned from the steps of the county courthouse to the highest bidder.

Not far from Lynch's pen stood a larger enclosure that housed children, some as young as five years old. Occasionally their mothers stayed with them until the youngsters were purchased, not through the pen owner's kindness, but to keep them from crying.

From the moment of young George's birth, Lizzie's rebellious behavior ceased. Although she had not wanted him, she loved him and cared about his future. She would do whatever was necessary to keep them together.

All black people were treated with suspicion in St. Louis. Patrols stood in the streets, each man armed with a pistol, a club, and a whip. They greeted white people but demanded a written pass from slaves and a fifteen-dollar license from free Negroes, one that permitted them to remain in the city. Patrolmen would rip shirts or dresses from the backs of those who lacked official documents and whip them before carting them off to jail.

One of the things Lizzie resented most about being a slave was her lack of formal education. Although she had learned the rudiments of reading and writing, she would be self-conscious about, and make excuses for, her lack of education for the rest of her life.

Free Negroes were not much better off than slaves. Although they paid school taxes, their children were forbidden to attend school. An 1847 Missouri law stated: "No person shall keep or teach any school for the instruction of negroes or mulattoes in reading or writing in this STATE." Punishment for breaking the law included a heavy fine, whipping at the public whipping post, and/or a six-month jail sentence.

Yet many black people found ways to educate their children. A few wealthy free Negroes sent their children to private schools in Northern states or to foreign countries. Others used illegal schools. Six Negro churches in St. Louis conducted "candle tallow schools" in their windowless basements. Tuition cost one dollar. No child, slave or free, was turned away for lack of money. Lizzie's son most likely attended one of the church's schools, for he was later accepted at Wilberforce University, a college for black students in Xenia, Ohio.

When unfriendly whites approached, a lookout signaled. Papers and spelling books were hidden, and Bibles or sewing appeared. Bible classes were considered legal because slaveowners often used biblical verse to convince slaves that their duty on earth was

Hugh A. Garland, Lizzie's master from 1840 until 1854. Steel engraving by J. C. Buttre. (BY PERMISSION OF THE MISSOURI HISTORICAL SOCIETY.)

to obey them. Slaveowners encouraged female slaves to become adept at sewing, a useful skill that increased their value.

But as far as Lizzie was concerned, there was no value in being a slave. The idea of gaining freedom for her son and herself had taken root in her mind long before she was consciously aware of it. Lizzie and her son could have escaped slavery through illegal means. One increasingly popular route was the Underground Railroad, a network of Negro and white abolitionists who helped runaway slaves to hide in coffins, under floorboards, in caves, or anyplace where they would be safe, until they could be moved to the next stop on their journey northward.

Entering a state that forbade slavery was another avenue to freedom. Lizzie often crossed the Mississippi River by ferry into the free state of Illinois, where she purchased fabric and trimmings for her patrons. But she always returned to Missouri and slavery. She didn't want to have to suffer the consequences if she were captured as a fugitive slave. Slave catchers hired by slaveowners often abducted fugitive slaves from free states and returned them to masters, who had them whipped, jailed, and then auctioned to the highest bidder. Advertisements for runaways appeared in daily newspapers and were hung on wooden billboards outside state and county buildings.

One ad read: "Negro girl called Mary. Has a small scar over eye, a good many teeth missing. The letter 'A' is branded on her cheek and forehead. $200 Reward."

Lizzie wanted freedom for her son, but she did not want him to live in fear of being captured and ending up in a worse situation than the one he had left. She would abide by the laws, no matter how unjust. She would buy their freedom. She tried to persuade her mother to join them, but the old woman refused. Born into the Burwell family of slaves, she had been present at the birth of each child. As they grew up, their hopes and dreams had become hers, and she basked in their joy and success and cried at their defeats.

One day Lizzie walked into Garland's study and informed him that she wished to buy herself and her son.

Without looking up from what he was doing, he waved her away with his hand and ordered her not to broach the subject again.

She refused to be put off and continued to make this request. One day, exasperated with her persistence, Garland angrily took a quarter from his pocket and thrust it toward her. Sarcastically, he said that if she really wanted to leave him, she should take the quarter to pay passage on the ferryboat that crossed the river to Illinois, where she and her son would be free. "It is the cheapest way that I know to accomplish what you desire," he said.

Lizzie answered immediately, "No, Master, I do not wish to be free in such a manner. I can cross the river anyday and have frequently done so, but will never leave in such a manner. By the laws of the land I am your slave. You are my master, and I will only be free by such means as the laws of the country provide."

Lizzie knew he liked her answer, but she was forced to let the matter rest because of circumstances beyond her control that threatened the lives of everyone in St. Louis and absorbed Garland's attention in that year of 1849.

CHAPTER FOUR

IN 1849, ONE of the worst cholera epidemics in the history of St. Louis killed four thousand people within seven months. Twelve thousand died within the year.

The Mississippi River, from which drinking water was drawn, had become contaminated by the sewage of thousands of men who stopped in St. Louis to equip themselves with mining gear on their way west to the California gold rush. Many of the Garlands' neighbors fled the city to stay with friends and relatives elsewhere. Others, including the Garlands, feared venturing from home. Dressmaking ceased, and Lizzie spent the year at home.

During the epidemic Garland became involved in a court case that at first seemed insignificant yet whose outcome would shake the foundation of the nation and change the course of history.

The slave Dred Scott, with the help of former boyhood friends who were white, sued his slaveowners, the Emersons, for his freedom on grounds that he had lived with Dr. Emerson in the free state of Illinois, which forbade slavery, while the doctor served in the military. A Missouri law permitted a slave to bring this type of suit against a white slaveholder. The principle of once free, always free, usually applied to slaves in Missouri. Dr. Emerson had since died, and Scott won his case against Mrs. Emerson in a lower court. Mrs. Emerson hired Garland to appeal the case to a higher court after her original attorney had died in the cholera epidemic.

Garland argued that because Dr. Emerson had been in the army when he took Scott into free territory, he was there not of his own free will but under military orders. And because military law superseded civil law, that made Scott still a slave. His argument won the appeal for Mrs. Emerson.

The case, however, would not be settled until 1857 after retrials and more appeals. Historians agree that the final decision by the Supreme Court not to grant Scott and his family freedom was probably one of the most powerful forces that brought about the Civil War.

The following year began with the cholera epidemic subsiding and the Garlands more dependent than ever upon Lizzie's income. The year brought a bitter battle over the

Dred Scott. In rejecting his claim to freedom, the Supreme Court sought to solve the slavery issue once and for all. Instead, its decision has been recorded as one of the most ill-advised and unfortunate moments in the court's history. Oil on canvas by Louis Schultze, circa 1881, from a photo, circa 1858. (BY PERMISSION OF THE MISSOURI HISTORICAL SOCIETY.)

question of extending slavery into six territories newly won from the war with Mexico: Texas, California, Arizona, New Mexico, Nevada, and Utah. As the new territories applied for statehood, strife erupted over whether they would be admitted as free or slave states. Slaveholders, fearful that more territories would apply as free rather than slave states, pressured congressmen to watch over their interests. To appease them, Congress passed the Compromise of 1850, which contained the Fugitive Slave Law. This law infuriated abolitionists of the North. It authorized U.S. marshals to gather posses of ordinary citizens and give them power to arrest suspected runaways. Not permitted to speak on their own behalf or have a trial, even free Negroes could be arrested and sold back into slavery. Anyone helping a fugitive could be fined one thousand dollars and sent to jail. Professional slave catchers opened offices in the North and advertised their services in Southern publications.

Thousands of former slaves and their families, who had successfully escaped years before, now fled their homes and jobs. Many relocated to Canada, where black men could vote, own property, and send their children to school.

The detested Fugitive Slave Law inspired Harriet Beecher Stowe to write *Uncle Tom's Cabin,* a novel that clearly showed the inseparability of cruelty and slavery.

Antislavery sentiment was gaining momentum. Garland, who was then writing a book on the history of slavery, must have realized that this institution might not survive, and that Lizzie and her son would leave him one way or another. One afternoon he summoned Lizzie to his study and said, "I've reconsidered, Lizzie. You have erved my family faithfully. You deserve your freedom. I will take $1,200 for you and your boy."

Although Lizzie didn't know how she could accumulate that much money, she remembered the moment all her life. She wrote, "Hope gave a silver lining to the dark cloud of my life—faint, it is true, but still a silver lining."

In 1852, with hope for future freedom, Lizzie married the man who had proposed to her years before, James Keckley. The ceremony was conducted by the Garlands' minister in their parlor, and Lizzie wore the bridal gown she had made for Mary Garland six months before.

With dreams of liberty on the horizon, Lizzie worked harder than ever. She continued to live with the Garlands while her husband rented a room across town.

Unfortunately, Lizzie's hopes for freedom dimmed as months turned into years and she was unable to save any money. The Garlands needed her earnings to meet their living expenses. Even worse, Lizzie discovered that her husband had lied to her. He was not a free man but a slave who belonged to a master in Virginia. Whatever little they had, he spent on whiskey. When she confronted him, he promised to reform. But time and again he failed to keep his word.

Things changed in 1854. Garland died unexpectedly, and a brother of Mrs. Garland's came to St. Louis from Vicksburg, Mississippi, to look after Garland's estate. Although Garland left no will, Mrs. Garland's brother knew of his brother-in-law's promise to Lizzie and assured her he would not prevent her from buying freedom.

Unable to save the twelve hundred dollars she

needed, Lizzie planned to borrow the sum from an abolitionist society in New York that lent slaves money to
purchase freedom. But when Lizzie asked Mrs. Garland's
permission to travel to New York, she was shocked when
she answered, "Lizzie, now that I am alone I must take
special care of my property." And Mrs. Garland de-

SLAVES' NAMES

Most slaves had no last names. It was customary for them
to have only a first name and be called by their owner's
last name. Lizzie was known as the Burwells' Lizzie. Slaves'
names changed when their masters changed. When Lizzie
went to live with the Garlands, she became known as the
Garlands' Lizzie.

All too often, unwanted sex was forced upon slave
women by their owners or by white overseers on plantations.
And the babies born of these improper (and unwanted)
unions became the property of their mother's master and
were given a first name preceded by their master's last name.

Lizzie's son, though fathered by a white man named Alexander Kirkland, was officially known only as Garland's
George. After she purchased her freedom, Lizzie took her
husband's name, Keckley, and in later years she began using
the middle name Hobbs, after the name of the man who was
her mother's husband. Not until later in her life did Lizzie
learn that Colonel Burwell was her actual father.

manded that Lizzie secure the names of six prominent gentlemen to vouch for her return—if she failed to return, they would pay Mrs. Garland twelve hundred dollars.

Lizzie chose six husbands from among her patrons. She was so sure of their support that she purchased a train ticket and packed her clothes before she called on them with her request. Obtaining the first five signatures was easy, but when Lizzie approached the husband of her sixth patron, he coldly replied, "Yes, yes, Lizzie. The scheme is a fair one and you shall have my name. But I shall bid you good-by when you start."

Lizzie was incredulous. "Surely you do not think I do not mean to return?" She could barely listen to his answer: "You mean to come back. That is, you mean to now, but you never will. When you reach New York, the abolitionists will tell you what savages we are, and they will convince you to stay and we shall never see you again."

Although Lizzie assured him he was mistaken, she would not accept his signature because he had no faith in her word.

The train for New York left without her.

When Mrs. LeBourgeois, another of Lizzie's patrons, learned of her failed attempt to gain freedom, she came by carriage to inform Lizzie she would raise twelve hundred dollars as a loan from Lizzie's many friends and patrons. Lizzie was touched by her kind gesture but dared not allow her hopes to be raised.

Within the next few weeks, however, Mrs. LeBourgeois made deposits at the bank of varying amounts until they finally totaled twelve hundred dollars. "Like a ray

Know all men by these presents, that I, Anne P. Garland of the County and City of St. Louis, State of Missouri, for and in consideration of the sum of twelve hundred dollars, to me in hand paid this day in cash, hereby emancipate my negro woman Lizzie and her son George — the said Lizzie is known in St. Louis, as the wife of James, who is called James Keckelly, is of light complexion, about thirty seven years of age, by trade a dress-maker, and called by those who know her, *Garland's Lizzie* — the said boy George, is the only child of Lizzie, is about sixteen years of age, and is almost white, and called by those who know him, *Garland's George*.

Witness my hand and seal, this 13th day of November A.D. 1855.

Witness   Anne P. Garland   (Seal)

John Wickham
Wily L. Williams

In St. Louis Circuit Court October Term 1855

November 18th 1855

State of Missouri }
County of St. Louis } ss.   Be it remembered that
on this fifteenth day of November Eighteen
hundred and fifty five In Open Court came
John Wickham & Wally L. Williams two subscribing
witnesses as examined under oath to that effect
proved the execution and Acknowledgment
of said deed by Anne P. Garland to Lizzie and
her son George which said proof of Acknow-
-ledgment is entered on the Record of the

Deed of emancipation of Lizzie and George Keckley. Photographer A. Garland. St. Louis Courthouse Papers. (BY PERMISSION OF THE MISSOURI HISTORICAL SOCIETY.)

of sunshine she came," wrote Lizzie, "and like a ray of sunshine she went away . . . at last my son and myself were free. Free, free! What a glorious ring to the word. Free! The bitter heart-struggle was over. . . . Free! The earth wore a brighter look, and the very stars seemed to sing with joy. Yes, free! Free by the laws of man and the smile of God—and Heaven bless them who made me so!"

*T*he ardent abolitionist John Brown, 1800–59.
(COURTESY OF THE LIBRARY OF CONGRESS.)

Lizzie moved in with her husband, although he continued to break his promises to reform. She retained most of her former clientele except for those who disapproved of slaves gaining freedom (they feared their own slaves might get the same idea).

Two of the young newly married Garland daughters, Mary and Carrie, whom Lizzie had taken special pride in dressing during their teenage years, died within a few months of each other, probably of either dysentery or cholera, both highly contagious deadly diseases that flourished at that time unchecked. Each daughter called for Lizzie and took her last breath in Lizzie's arms. Mrs. Garland moved to Vicksburg, Mississippi, taking Lizzie's mother with her. When Lizzie was later summoned there to her mother's deathbed, the ailing woman revealed that Colonel Burwell was Lizzie's real father. It is difficult to know how Lizzie reacted, but when she wrote her book several years later, she referred to George Pleasant Hobbs as the father she loved, and mentioned only in passing that her mother had revealed that her "real" father was the colonel.

After spending a few weeks with the Garland family in Vicksburg, Lizzie returned to St. Louis but was no longer content to remain there. Negative attitudes toward black people became even worse in 1859, perhaps because of John Brown's raid. An ardent abolitionist, John Brown and his followers attacked a huge federal arsenal at Harpers Ferry, Virginia, in an attempt to free the slaves. Although federal troops ended the rebellion and John Brown and his followers were hanged, more restrictive laws were passed throughout the South, including Missouri, aimed at curtailing freedom of *free* black people.

In the spring of 1860, with the same resolve that enabled her to survive and surmount the obstacles of slavery, Lizzie left her irresponsible husband and St. Louis for Baltimore, Maryland, armed with letters of recommendation from her patrons.

CHAPTER FIVE

IN BALTIMORE, LIZZIE started giving sewing classes for black girls (most likely through the African Methodist Episcopalian Church, where courses were offered to educate black children). Although there were more free Negroes in Maryland than in any other state, and although they paid $500 in public school taxes, their children were not permitted to attend public schools.

After struggling for nearly six weeks to attract enough paying students to meet her expenses, Lizzie failed and was forced to abandon her idea. With barely enough money for train fare, she left Baltimore for Washington, D.C.

No sooner had Lizzie found a job as an assistant dressmaker for two and a half dollars a day than she was notified that a city law demanded that a white person must vouch to authorities that she was free, and that she was required to purchase a fifteen-dollar license or leave the city within ten days. Fifteen dollars was more than Lizzie had at the time, and her salary was uncertain since it depended on the number of days she was called to work.

Lizzie explained her dilemma to Mrs. Rheingold, one of the women she sewed for, who knew important people in the government. She and Lizzie visited the mayor of Washington, who granted Lizzie special permission to remain in the city without a license and instructed the

The Walker Lewis Boardinghouse at 1017 Twelfth Street N.W., Washington, D.C. What is thought to be the original building is still standing. (PHOTO BY DR. FRANCES DIAMOND.)

police not to harass her.

Although Lizzie had debts to pay and no one to help her, she decided to open her own dressmaking business. She rented two small rooms in the rear of the Walker Lewis Boardinghouse on Twelfth Street, a good, safe neighborhood within walking distance of the White House. The Lewises were leading caterers in town and rented rooms to lodgers in their three-story house that stood next door to Madame Estern's beauty salon, where many wealthy Washington women had their hair done. To lend credence to her new venture, Lizzie ordered business cards and had a sign made.

Lizzie recalled her first days as a business owner: "Work came in slowly, and I was beginning to feel very much embarrassed, for I did not know how I was to meet bills staring me in the face . . . the bills were small, but they were formidable to me, who had little or nothing to pay them with."

Her son, George, now twenty-one, had worked and

helped to repay some of the cost of their freedom, but now he was in his freshman year at Wilberforce University and could no longer contribute money. Lizzie's husband, James Keckley, who had never contributed to their support, died in St. Louis some time after she left him.

Some of the women Lizzie had sewn for while working as an assistant dressmaker became her first patrons. One day while she was in the home of Mrs. Rheingold to fit a dress, she met the wife of Captain Robert E. Lee, who was visiting. Mrs. Lee needed a gown suitable for the great event of the season, soon to take place—a dinner party given at the White House in honor of the Prince of Wales. She had purchased silk fabric but hadn't found a suitable dressmaker. She hired Lizzie.

When Lizzie called on her the next day, Mrs. Lee's husband, Captain Lee, handed her one hundred dollars and asked that she spare no expense in purchasing suitable trimmings for the dress. Captain Lee would later be known as the famous General Robert E. Lee, commander of the Confederate troops, in the war that would soon divide the nation.

Lizzie entered Harper & Mitchell's Dry Goods Store on Pennsylvania Avenue and asked to look at their laces. When she asked Mr. Harper if she could take the laces for Mrs. Lee's approval, he readily agreed. His trust of her moved her to remind him she was a stranger and the goods were valuable. He remarked that he believed her face was an index to an honest heart. Lizzie never forgot his kind words.

Lizzie finished the dress on time, and Mrs. Lee attracted favorable attention at the event. After that eve-

PROBLEMS OF THE MANTUA

Only those dressmakers able to make the mantua, the difficult-to-sew but popular dress of the eighteenth and nineteenth centuries, were called mantuamakers. The bodice of the dress fit snugly through pleats stitched in the back to the waist. Novice mantuamakers took apart old mantuas or their linings and used them as patterns for new ones. As they became more adept and experienced, they measured individual pieces directly on their patrons. They then cut and sewed them by hand.

The skirt of the mantua draped over a cone-shaped understructure that ended in a hoop made from whalebone or metal. The circumference of the skirt could be as wide as eighteen feet and could require as many as twenty-five yards of material.

Mantuamakers could do some creative and elaborate trimming on the vast amount of material the dress required. Lace, feathers, ribbons, flounces, fringes, flowers, vines and leaves, appliqués, buttons, and embroidery embellished mantuas. At the same time, the outfit presented serious fitting problems. A patron might stand erect at one fitting and stoop or lean to one side at the next fitting; she might lose or gain weight from one fitting to the next. Fashionable ladies sought an hourglass look with a fifteen-inch waistline. Wearing a different corset, lacing it looser or tighter would throw off the precise measurements. Women needed help dressing, and when their corset lacings were pulled too tight, they fainted. Fashionably furnished rooms included swooning couches.

Mantuas presented other problems. They filled a room quickly, and when women moved in certain ways their skirts tilted up on one side and down on the other, exposing embarrassing views of their legs and undergarments. Sometimes when the hoop got crushed, it bent at odd angles, causing the skirt to lie askew. The dresses' girth kept men at a distance, caused garments to catch fire when women stood too close to a lighted fireplace, and prevented one woman from coming to the aid of another. It took just a few mantuas to fill the space in stagecoaches, and sometimes material from the skirt became tangled in wagon wheels and that caused traffic jams. New York omnibuses charged higher fares for women with hoops.

Despite the inconveniences of multiple fittings, difficulty in dressing, and awkwardness and hazards of moving around in the garment—not to mention its high cost—mantuas were all the rage. And highly fashionable ladies couldn't be seen twice in the same mantua.

ning, Lizzie received many orders and was soon able to pay most of her bills.

On her travels about Washington, she heard that Mrs. Varina Howell Davis, wife of Jefferson Davis, the sena-

*S*ketch of an 1860 evening dress from the Journal des Demoiselles, *drawn by Dr. L. David Rutberg.*

tor from Mississippi, was looking for a mantuamaker. Lizzie visited her home and left one of her business cards. Mrs. Davis hired her on the spot.

Lizzie spent every afternoon at the Davises' fitting and sewing many outfits. In her presence the Davises freely discussed the prospect of war between the slave-

Varina Howell Davis, wife of Jefferson Davis, Southern statesman and president of the Confederacy. (COURTESY OF THE MASSACHUSETTS COMMANDERY MILITARY ORDER OF THE LOYAL LEGION AND THE U.S. ARMY MILITARY HISTORY INSTITUTE.)

holding South and the abolitionist North. Servants and family members told Lizzie about secret meetings held at the house every night.

Lizzie's fashionable creations drew more and more praise; her business grew rapidly, and patrons included wives of senators, congressmen, and Cabinet members. With the approach of her first Christmas in the nation's capital, she could barely fill all the orders placed with her.

At fifteen minutes before twelve on Christmas Eve, 1860, in the Davis home, Lizzie sat in a room next to the one where the family trimmed their Christmas tree. Lizzie arranged the last cords on a dressing gown Mrs. Davis had ordered as a present for her husband. As the clock struck twelve, Lizzie finished the last stitch, unaware, of course, that Mr. Davis would wear it often as president of the Confederate states during the upcoming struggle between the North and the South.

War became certain before the end of January. While Lizzie was dressing Mrs. Davis one day, her patron invited her to move south with the Davis family. She assured Lizzie that the Southern states would be victorious after a brief fight and that Mr. Davis would be elected president of all the states. She planned to live in the White House and promised to hire Lizzie.

Ever since arriving in Washington and her first glimpse of the White House, Lizzie had nurtured a dream of working for the women there. To fulfill that dream, she was ready to make almost any sacrifice. She refused Mrs. Davis's offer, however. She was vehemently against the South's plan to extend slavery into the new territories, and she had faith in the strength of the North. She would not compromise her beliefs. A few weeks before Mrs. Davis left for the South, Lizzie made two inexpensive plain chintz wrappers for her. Mrs. Davis explained that she planned to stop wearing expensive clothes for a while now that war was inevitable. Lizzie would see those same chintz wrappers at another time in another place, after much of the nation's blood had been shed. Mrs. Davis left some delicate needlework with Lizzie to finish and asked her to forward it to Montgomery, Alabama, where she and her family planned to be.

By the end of February, Jefferson Davis had been elected president of seven Southern states that had formally seceded from the Union, and Abraham Lincoln had been elected president of the Union. It was about that time that one of Lizzie's patrons, Mrs. John McClean, needed a gown made on very short notice and promised to introduce Lizzie to Mrs. Lincoln and recommend her services as a mantuamaker.

CHAPTER SIX

LIZZIE WAS THE last dressmaker to be called for an interview at the White House with Mrs. Lincoln. Nervously, she climbed the steps to the Family Room, where she found Mary Todd Lincoln dressed in a cashmere wraparound morning robe, standing by a window. Mrs. Lincoln turned, smiled, and walked toward her. Lizzie had heard rumors that the new president's wife was vulgar and ignorant. She felt pleasantly surprised when Mrs. Lincoln greeted her cordially: "Mrs. Keckley, you have come at last."

Mrs. Lincoln asked for references and seemed most impressed when Lizzie named Mrs. Jefferson Davis as one of her patrons. Lizzie presented several letters of recommendations from former St. Louis clients and discovered some were friends of Mrs. Lincoln.

When Mrs. Lincoln asked if Lizzie could do her work, she answered almost inaudibly, "Yes." Then, more boldly, she asked, "Will you have much work for me to do?"

Mrs. Lincoln replied, "That, Mrs. Keckley, will depend altogether upon your prices. I trust your terms are reasonable. I cannot afford to be extravagant. We are just from the west and are poor. If you do not charge too much, I shall be able to give you all my work."

Lizzie made her terms very reasonable, and Mrs. Lincoln handed her a bright-colored antique rose silk gown that she planned to wear to the first White House reception that Friday night. It needed altering. Lizzie measured her and took the gown home.

Lizzie was hard at work in her rooms finishing the alterations when word came that the affair was going to be postponed until the following Tuesday. Lizzie heaved a sigh of relief now that she had more time to complete the gown. However, Mrs. Lincoln soon sent for her and asked that she change the entire style of the dress. And she also ordered a blue silk blouse for her cousin, Elizabeth

Mary Todd Lincoln, circa 1862, portrait by Mathew Brady. This "wartime card portrait" was widely published in periodicals. (USED BY PERMISSION OF THE LLOYD OSTENDORF COLLECTION, DAYTON, OHIO.)

Grimsley. Although Lizzie was swamped with other orders, she knew she had to meet these last-minute demands. Mrs. Lincoln had to be pleased no matter how inconvenient her requests.

Tuesday evening Lizzie put the last stitches in the dress, folded and carried it and the finished blue blouse to the White House. When she entered the family quarters, there were several women gathered about Mrs. Lincoln, all talking at once. Above the others, Lizzie heard Mrs. Lincoln's distraught voice, complaining that she could not attend the reception because she had nothing to wear.

She turned, saw Lizzie, and snarled, "Mrs. Keckley, you have disappointed me—deceived me. Why do you bring my dress at this late hour?"

"Because I have just finished it, and I thought I should be in time," Lizzie answered, her hopes and dreams fading before her.

"But you are not in time, Mrs. Keckley; you have bitterly disappointed me. I have no time to dress and, what is more, I will not dress and go down-stairs."

Lizzie did not think she was late. In the past her seasoned hands took little time to dress her patrons and arrange their hair. She said, "I am sorry if I have disappointed you, Mrs. Lincoln, for I intended to be on time. Will you let me dress you? I can have you ready in a few minutes."

Mrs. Lincoln sputtered, "No, I won't be dressed. I will stay in my room. Mr. Lincoln can go down with the other ladies."

The women in the room pleaded with Mrs. Lincoln to allow Lizzie to dress her. After more protestations, she finally relented. Lizzie was used to placating highstrung white women. They often aimed their insecurities and nervousness at those serving them. Lizzie calmly dressed Mrs. Lincoln and wove fresh flowers grown in the White House conservatory into her hair. The dress fit well, and Mrs. Lincoln seemed pleased. Lizzie breathed a sigh of relief.

President Lincoln entered the room with two of his sons, ten-year-old Willie and eight-year-old Tad. He threw himself on the sofa, laughed, pulled on his white

Lincoln family portrait: Mrs. Lincoln, Willie, Robert, Tad, and President Lincoln. Painting by Francis B. Carpenter, circa 1861. (COURTESY OF THE LIBRARY OF CONGRESS.)

gloves, and began reciting poetry. He looked appraisingly at Mrs. Lincoln and said, "I declare, you look charming in that dress. Mrs. Keckley has met with great success." Lizzie must have felt deeply satisfied by the compliment, but in her heart she knew it was his wife who had to be pleased.

Just before President and Mrs. Lincoln descended the stairway to the first White House levee—a presidential reception—Tad, as a prank, hid his mother's lace handkerchief. When she became unstrung for the second time that evening, he returned it.

Lizzie was surprised when instead of being embarrassed by her uncontrolled outburst, Mrs. Lincoln took the President's arm and led the party downstairs as if nothing had happened. Lizzie wrote in her memoirs, "No queen, accustomed to . . . royalty all her life, could have comported herself with more calmness and dignity than did the wife of the President. She was confident and self possessed."

The first reception was a huge success, and Mrs. Lincoln received many compliments on her gown. Lizzie's anxieties turned to joy and relief as she officially became Mrs. Lincoln's mantuamaker.

Mary Todd Lincoln is one of the most controversial characters in American history. She grew up as a pampered Southern belle in Lexington, Kentucky, but when she was six and a half, her mother died. Her father quickly began courting another woman and remarried. He and his second wife had nine children. Mary was left to fend for herself or to seek comfort and love from Mammy Sally, a Todd family slave. Mary was better educated than most women of her day. At fourteen she entered the exclusive Mentelle's Boarding School, where she became fluent in French, well versed in current events, knowledgeable about international affairs, and adept at dancing the most fashionable steps of the day. She excelled in her studies, won prizes, and sparkled as the life of any party. When she left school, she attended parties, teas, lectures, and rode sidesaddle on horseback. She loved to debate political matters with her father's distinguished visitors, behavior considered outlandish for a proper Southern lady. Her biting wit and sharp tongue put many people on edge. Etiquette of the day dictated that proper females should be good listeners, perhaps apt questioners, but they should not join men's discussions and should *never* voice an opinion. Etiquette also dictated that a woman's name should appear in the newspaper only twice: in the announcement of her marriage and in the notice of her death.

Mary Todd met Abe Lincoln after fleeing her father's and stepmother's home in Kentucky where she and her siblings battled with their stepmother and her children. She moved to Springfield, Illinois, to live with her older sister, Elizabeth. Elizabeth was married to Ninian Edwards, a respected political leader and son of a former governor of Kentucky. They made their grand hillside home the center of frequent gatherings of the most socially prominent people in Springfield. Elizabeth greeted their guests in French.

Springfield had become the state's capital in 1839, the year Mary came to live there. The state's most promising political figures, many of whom were bachelors, lived there, as did the most marriageable young women in Illinois. They were considered to be either socially or politically very worthwhile and were invited to every ball and party. The group became known as the "Coterie."

Abe had moved to Springfield from Salem as an elected delegate to the state legislature and had opened a law practice with John Todd Stuart, a cousin to Mary. Although he was unschooled; ill at ease with women; dressed in skimpy swallowtail coats, shabby patched trousers, socks that rarely matched; and failed to measure up to the educated and socially skilled guests that made up the "Coterie," he was included in their clique because of his position. It is believed he met Mary at one of their balls.

When she eventually wed Abraham Lincoln, Mary's affluent family felt she'd married beneath her status. At the time he and Mary were married, Abe Lincoln was considered by many to be "a poor nobody." But Mary loved him and sensed his potential greatness. Even though they were relatively poor after they married, Mary continued to love amusement and pretty clothes. She fought over pennies with ice and berry vendors so she could save money to buy herself fine things.

Mary Lincoln seemed to undergo a personality change after she married Abe. From the comfortable life of a wealthy belle, cared for by servants, courted and fawned over by the most eligible bachelors in Springfield, she seemed overwhelmed with the responsibilities of a wife and mother. Immediately after their marriage, they moved to the Globe Tavern, a noisy, crowded, and confining hotel-boardinghouse. They lived and ate meals there, paying four dollars a week, until after the birth of their son, Robert Todd, just nine months after they were married. They soon moved to a rented three-room cottage and then to a more spacious home in Springfield, but Mary seemed unable to cope with the added chores of a larger home, not to mention the births of three more children, Eddy, Willie, and Tad, and a husband gone from home six months each year. (Abe rode a circuit trying cases in outlying districts.) When Abe was home, men and political affairs absorbed him. Mary's growing insecurity about her worth as a person, the added stress of new responsibilities, catastrophic events, such as the death of Eddie, and her growing fears of pending doom drove her to do and say things that shocked people. She seldom held her tongue.

When the Lincolns lived in Springfield, Illinois, tales gathered and spread about Mrs. Lincoln. Once, while a colleague visited her husband, she shouted that she felt neglected, abused, and insulted. Then she slammed the door. During thunderstorms, she was so fearful and nervous, Mr. Lincoln would hurry home from his law office to calm her. When Mrs. Lincoln was alone and under stress, she often had chills, headaches, and fears that sometimes turned into hallucinations. Once, when her husband traveled his law circuit, she wept and wailed loudly enough for neighbors to hear. She believed some rough characters had their eyes on her and her hired girl. She asked Mr. Gourley, the Lincolns' next-door neighbor, to spend the night at her house.

Known to be hard to please, Mrs. Lincoln discharged a household servant after reducing the girl to tears with a tongue-lashing. When the girl's uncle complained to Mr. Lincoln about Mrs. Lincoln's treatment of his niece, Mr. Lincoln soberly replied, "If I have had to stand this every day for fifteen years, don't you think you can stand it a few minutes one day?" Without his wife's knowledge, Mr. Lincoln paid one servant an extra dollar a week to put up with Mrs. Lincoln's demands.

When Abe Lincoln was elected president and the couple moved to the capital, Mrs. Lincoln was stunned by the hostility of Washington society. She was ignored by most of the influential women in the political arena and treated as if she were a country bumpkin, not worthy to be a president's wife.

CHAPTER SEVEN

ANGER BETWEEN THE North and the South over the question of extending slavery into the new territories reached a climax on April 12, 1861, when Southern troops attacked Union soldiers at Fort Sumter, a federal arsenal located on an island in the harbor of South Carolina. Two days later, the Union troops at the fort were forced to haul down the Stars and Stripes. The next day, President Lincoln summoned 75,000 men to volunteer as soldiers for three months. He believed strong Northern forces would end the conflict within days.

Lizzie should not have been surprised when on April 24, her son, George, left Wilberforce University during his freshman year to be among the first to volunteer for the three-month service. Now known as George Kirkland—he had adopted the surname of his white father, who had died when George was just eighteen months old—he was willing to sacrifice his life fighting *against* everything Alexander Kirkland had stood for. George enlisted as a white man in the First Missouri Volunteers and became a private.

Although thousands of black men volunteered to fight, their offer was stoutly rejected. President Lincoln feared that the border states of Missouri, Kentucky, Maryland, and Delaware, where slavery was accepted and practiced but where pro-Union feeling was strong, would join the Confederacy if he armed the blacks.

At this time, Mrs. Lincoln was a staunch abolitionist. In fact, some historians believe Mrs. Lincoln convinced her husband of the need to free the slaves long before he actually did so. The first lady had not always been against slavery. Just five years before, she had sent her cousin a letter apologizing for Mr. Lincoln's allegiance to the Republican Party. She had assured her that Mr. Lincoln was not an abolitionist and then noted that having a few cowering Negroes about the house might be preferable to dealing with "wild Irish" help.

Why the change of heart? Many historians believe it was due to Lizzie's influence.

Mrs. Lincoln turned more and more to Lizzie as a friend and confidante as her husband became increasingly absorbed with the war and paid less attention to her. She sought out Lizzie for comfort, the same way she had run to her mammy, Sally, for comfort as a child.

When young Willie and Tad caught the measles in May of 1861, Mrs. Lincoln, being new to Washington, knew few people she could call upon for aid. Lizzie volunteered to care for the boys, and Mrs. Lincoln came to depend on her for help with their care.

Lizzie made Mrs. Lincoln fifteen or sixteen dresses during her first spring in the White House. She learned that the first lady's favorite color was white but that she also liked pink, deep purples, bright yellows, royal blues, and crimson. She preferred low-cut gowns with short sleeves that showed off her smooth neck and arms. Pearls were her favorite jewelry.

Along with Mrs. Lincoln's activities as first lady, Lizzie's creations made news. On May 10, 1861, the *Chicago Tribune* reported on a reception Mrs. Lincoln had given

Mary Todd Lincoln, January 1862, portrait by Mathew Brady. (COURTESY OF THE LIBRARY OF CONGRESS.)

the previous day. "Mrs. Lincoln wore a very elegant blue silk, richly embroidered, with a long train; also point lace cape, and a full set of pearl ornaments, in which she well sustained the dignity of her station."

When Mrs. Lincoln gave a dinner party for Prince Napoleon of France, the *New York Herald* reported that she was "simply but tastefully attired in white."

Lizzie became the most popular dressmaker in Washington and had so many orders, she had to rent a large workroom across from her boardinghouse. She employed as many as twenty assistants.

Mary Clemmer Ames, a prolific Civil War journalist in one of her articles called Mrs. Keckley

a stately, stylish woman, cheek tawny, features regular . . . a face strong with intellect and heart . . . It is Lizzie who fashions those splendid costumes of Mrs. Lincoln, whose artistic elegance has been so highly praised during the last winter. Stately carriages stand before her door, whose haughty owners sit before Lizzie docile as lambs, whilst she tells them what to wear. Lizzie is an artist, and has such a genius for making women look pretty that no one thinks of disputing her decrees.

Lizzie dressed Mrs. Lincoln for each White House occasion, wove fresh flowers into her hair, arranged her bouquets, and saw that her gloves were pulled taut. Lizzie's hands were the last to touch her before she took the arm of the president and descended the stairs to the great social events of the day.

Lizzie also groomed the president. Many times he would turn to her and say, "Madam 'Lizabeth, would you comb my unruly bristles down to-night?" His habit of running his fingers through his coarse hair often made him look untidy. He would relax in his easy chair as Lizzie took his brush and comb and straightened his tousled hair.

When the North suffered a disastrous defeat in the first major battle at Bull Run, just twenty miles or so outside Washington, rumors circulated that the city was to be attacked at any time. The nation's capital grew increasingly tense as the war continued, and it was obvious that the fighting would not cease in three months.

DISEASES

More Americans lost their lives from disease in the Civil War than from bullets. Of the more than half million who died, two out of three lost their lives in army camps from epidemics of typhoid, malaria, yellow fever, diphtheria, cholera, dysentery, diarrhea, pneumonia, measles, mumps, and chicken pox. Owing to a lack of sanitary and healthful conditions, soldiers were forced to drink polluted water, and to eat a diet that included rancid meat and excluded fresh vegetables. From fear of being shot with their trousers down, soldiers often relieved their bowels within a few feet of their tents. Mosquitoes, lice, mites, and fleas flourished and passed on diseases.

Typhoid and dysentery bacteria entered the body through contaminated food or water, while mosquitoes spread malaria and yellow fever. Diphtheria thrived through direct contact with someone who carried the bacteria or with someone who had an active case. Cholera, caused by poor sanitation and polluted water, resulted in the most discomfort and the highest number of deaths. The disease caused massive diarrhea—with a loss of three or four gallons of liquid and salts in twenty-four hours—followed by vomiting. Patients quickly became dehydrated, lapsed into a coma, and often died. Measles, mumps, chicken pox, and pneumonia ran rampant among underfed, poorly clothed, and overly fatigued soldiers in crowded tents with muddy floors and poor ventilation. It is estimated that the Civil War was prolonged by two years because disease interrupted planned battles.

Few advances in medical care had been made since Revolutionary War days. The theory that germs cause disease had not yet been discovered, and antibiotics were unknown. One surgeon was assigned to care for one thousand men in unsanitary, makeshift, poorly equipped hospitals. Few drugs were available, and some of them (e.g., arsenic, strychnine, and calomel) were actually poisonous. Within the space of one year, the average soldier was sick enough to be sent to the hospital two or three times. Being sent to the hospital often proved more dangerous than fighting on the battlefield.

Thousands and thousands of new volunteers arrived weekly. Ragged-looking men dressed in a variety of tattered clothes who had not eaten in days passed by Lizzie's windows. They were quartered wherever room could be found for them, including the floors and seats in the Senate, the House of Representatives, and the halls of the White House. Basement furnaces were used to cook bacon, bread, and coffee.

With the added burden of soldiers, malaria and dysentery spread through the city, especially during the summer months. The Washington Canal emitted ghastly nighttime odors. Army camps without latrine trenches

The Battle of Lexington at Wilson's Creek, Missouri, where Lizzie's son, George Kirkland, was killed on August 10, 1861. This pen-and-ink sketch by Henri Lovie was made on the spot for Frank Leslie's Illustrated Newspaper. (BY PERMISSION OF THE GENERAL RESEARCH DIVISION OF THE NEW YORK PUBLIC LIBRARY, ASTOR, LENOX, AND TILDEN FOUNDATIONS.)

lined the banks of the Potomac River. By mid-August the river had become an ugly, smelly waste receptacle, and its poisonous water was piped back into those homes that had running water, including the White House. After the war was over, it was reported that more soldiers died from disease than from bullets.

Mrs. Lincoln became so ill with chills and fever her first summer in Washington that President Lincoln persuaded her to go north to Saratoga, New York, and Long Branch, New Jersey, until the cold weather set in. Mineral waters there were supposed to have curative powers.

While Mrs. Lincoln vacationed, Lizzie received dreaded news that her son, George, had been killed on August 10 in the Battle of Lexington at Wilson's Creek, Missouri. Lizzie's grief was intensified because she could not give him a proper funeral. She had no grave to visit. His remains probably lay alongside those of thousands of others killed on the battlefield, and buried in shallow unmarked graves near where they had fallen.

Mr. Lincoln must have written to Mrs. Lincoln about young George's death, because she sent Lizzie a condolence letter from New York. Lizzie appreciated the gesture, saying, "The kind womanly letter that Mrs. Lincoln wrote to me when she heard of my bereavement was full of golden words of comfort."

In a letter dated September 29, Mrs. Lincoln informed her cousin of the sad news: "I know you will be sorry to hear that our colored mantuamaker, Elizabeth, lost her only son and child in the battle of Lexington, Missouri. She is heartbroken. She is a remarkable woman herself."

While Lizzie grieved, the *New York Herald* reported late in August that Mrs. Lincoln had attended a grand ball at Long Branch in "an elegant robe of white grenadine with a long flowing train, the bottom skirt puffed with quilling of white satin, and the apron and shoulders uncovered, save with an elegant point lace shawl. She wore a necklace and bracelets of superb pearls, a pearl fan, and headdress of wreathed wild roses. Beyond all comparison she was the most richly and completely dressed lady present."

Reporters as well as abolitionists began to object to Mrs. Lincoln's behavior. She traveled unescorted, attended dances without her husband, and seemingly ig-

Mary Todd Lincoln, in the dress believed to be the one on which Lizzie sewed sixty bows and hundreds of dots. Portrait by Mathew Brady circa 1862. (COURTESY OF THE LIBRARY OF CONGRESS.)

nored the war effort when it needed her the most. The press focused especially on her shopping trips.

Mary Clemmer Ames wrote that "while sister women scraped lint, sewed bandages and put on nurses' caps and gave their all to their country including their husbands and sons, the wife of the President spent her time rolling to and fro between Washington and New York, intent on making extravagant purchases for the White House and herself."

Along with the purchase of eighty-four pairs of gloves, a three-thousand-dollar shawl, and a four-thousand-dollar earrings-and-pin set, Mrs. Lincoln bought several pairs of draperies for the White House at her favorite spot, the Ladies' Mile in New York, where the most fashionable and expensive shops in the country were located. Congress had allotted her twenty thousand dollars to refurbish the White House; she had already spent twenty-seven thousand dollars.

Mrs. Lincoln returned from Saratoga and Long Branch in November and brought several yards of fine cloth and trimmings for Lizzie to sew. She asked Lizzie to tack sixty bows and hundreds of black dots onto an off-the-shoulder heavy white silk gown she planned to wear for a portrait taken by Mathew Brady, a prominent Civil War photographer.

In addition to the needs and demands of Mrs. Lincoln, the unruly behavior of the young Lincoln boys, Willie and Tad, distracted Lizzie and helped her cope with her grief. The boys could turn up under desks, behind draperies, in the basement, even on the roof. They played jokes on unsuspecting victims and frightened everyone when they set off the central White House bell system that signaled extreme emergency. They attached pet goats to carts, rode through crowds of people in the East Room, and sneaked the animals onto an elevator and into Tad's room, where one was later found sleeping in his bed. Sometimes the only people who laughed at these pranks were the president, Mrs. Lincoln, and Lizzie.

Unfortunately, the merriment the boys brought to the mansion soon ended, and the criticism aimed at their mother increased with a vengeance.

Mrs. Lincoln had planned a large reception for five hundred people on February 5, 1862, and had sent out invitations in January. She hired Maillard's, the most expensive caterers in the country, for the event.

As the day drew near, Willie became ill and Mrs. Lincoln wanted to cancel the party. Willie's physician, however, assured her he was recuperating.

On the night of the party, Willie grew worse. Mrs. Lincoln sat by his bedside and held his hand. Lizzie promised to watch over him while the president's wife entertained her guests.

After Lizzie finished dressing Mrs. Lincoln in an elegant white satin gown with a long ruffled train, Mr. Lincoln entered the room. He stared at his wife's bare arms and neck, looked at the dress a few minutes, then said, "Whew! Our cat has a long tail to-night."

When Mrs. Lincoln made no reply, he added, "Mother, it is my opinion, if some of that tail was nearer the head, it would be in better style."

Lizzie watched Mrs. Lincoln hide a faint smile, take the president's arm, and slowly walk downstairs to the reception.

Lizzie sat by Willie's bed throughout the evening, bathing his burning forehead with cool water. She could hear the music the Marine Band played as guests arrived at the gaily lit courtyard in carriages and ambulances. Most vehicles in Washington had been converted to makeshift ambulances and there were few conveyances left for private use, so ambulances were used to transport guests to social occasions.

During the evening Mrs. Lincoln left the reception several times to check on Willie. Although Lizzie reassured her he would be all right, each time she left his bedside she became more worried about him.

The festivity attracted widespread newspaper coverage. An article in the *Washington Star* stated that "the party was the most superb affair of its kind ever seen here. No expense was spared."

The public was outraged to read that ambulances had transported guests to an elaborate White House party while desperately ill men suffered in cold, roofless makeshift hospitals without heat on straw or dirt beds covered with snow instead of blankets.

A Philadelphia poet wrote a scorching ode entitled "The Queen Must Dance." Although there was no dancing and Willie had become ill *after* the invitations had been sent, the people and the press blamed Mary Lincoln for her son's illness. Lizzie seethed with indignation over the unjustified attacks. People needed to know the true story. She wished she could set them straight.

The senior senator from Oregon, James Nesmith, ridiculed Mrs. Lincoln in a letter he wrote to his wife that night: "Weak minded Mrs. Lincoln and her sorry show of skin and bones. She had her bosom on exhibition, a flowerpot on her head—There was a train of silk dragging on the floor behind her of several yards in length."

Willie lingered for nearly two weeks after the party, then fell into a coma and died two days later. Lizzie, exhausted from caring for him day and night, was not by his side but was sent for immediately.

Mrs. Lincoln collapsed with grief. She lay writhing

in bed, sobbing uncontrollably. Lizzie bathed her temples with cool water. Only six months before, Lizzie had lost George. She understood a mother's grief.

Lizzie dressed Willie's body in evening attire for his funeral. She placed in his lifeless hands a bouquet of flowers sent by his bedridden mother. Lizzie would remove them before his burial and press them for Mrs. Lincoln.

Lizzie stood at the foot of Willie's bed when President Lincoln entered the room. She watched him, bent with grief as he lifted the cover from his son's face and gazed at it for a long time. In her book, she wrote that he said, "My poor boy, he was too good for this earth. God has called him home. I know that he is much better off in heaven, but then we loved him so. It is hard, hard to have him die!" Deep sobs choked his words. He buried his head in his hands; his body shook with grief.

Tears filled Lizzie's eyes. She stared in silent awe, marveling that such a man, so rugged and strong, could be so moved. Lizzie wrote, "With me that picture of Mr. Lincoln is immortal—I really believe that I shall carry it with me across the dark, mysterious river of death."

Mrs. Lincoln never again entered the Guest Room where her son had died, nor the Green Room where Lizzie had prepared his body for burial. Mary Lincoln destroyed all signs of him and refused to look at his photograph. She sent most of his possessions to Springfield, Illinois, where Willie had spent many happy days before their move to Washington.

The president and his eldest son, Robert, a student home from Harvard University, accompanied Willie's body to the nearby cemetery, while Lizzie sat by Mrs. Lincoln, who lay in a darkened room and wept all day.

Signs of mourning appeared everywhere. Black crepe covered all the mirrors, pictures, and door frames of the White House. Mrs. Lincoln canceled the marine concerts held on the White House lawn every Wednesday and Saturday as a pleasant diversion for the public from the grimness of war. Balls and receptions stopped. Orders for gowns ceased, and Lizzie was so busy nursing Mrs. Lincoln that she had little time for anything else. Fortunately ᵢfor Lizzie, she was paid through congressional funds for her care of the Lincoln family.

Mrs. Lincoln lay sobbing in bed over Willie's death for three weeks. Her weeping caused a persistent sore throat, blurry eyesight, shaking, and weakness; Willie had similar symptoms before he died. One day weeks after Willie's funeral, Lizzie reported that while she tended Mrs. Lincoln, Mr. Lincoln bent over his wife's bed, took her gently by the arm, and led her to the window. He pointed to the insane asylum in the distance and said, "Mother, do you

Mrs. Lincoln in the first stage of mourning for Willie Lincoln in 1862. (COURTESY OF THE LIBRARY OF CONGRESS.)

see that large white building on the hill yonder? Try and control your grief, or it will drive you mad, and we may have to send you there."

Despite their personal grief, on April 16 President Lincoln signed the bill that emancipated more than 3,000 slaves in Washington. The act was a blow to slavery everywhere, and Negroes throughout the country celebrated. Negro churches held special services where the people sang, danced, wept, shouted, and prayed.

For more than a year after Willie's death, Mary Lincoln wore black mourning clothes, even though the custom called for wearing black for only six months. Her headgear was so rigidly constructed, she was unable to turn her head. She wore jet-black jewelry. She used writing paper bordered with very thick black margins.

Eventually, Mrs. Lincoln dressed in half-mourning colors of lavender, gray, and somber purples with a bit of white, colors denoting the next stage of grief.

To help Mrs. Lincoln cope with her loss, Lizzie introduced her to spiritualists. Mrs. Lincoln became a believer almost immediately. She and Lizzie attended séances where spiritualists summoned the dead to speak with their loved ones. Mary Lincoln claimed to have spoken with her dead son, Willie, and to have seen her other dead son, Eddy, who had died at the age of four in Springfield many years before. The president accompanied his wife on several occasions, and one séance is known to have been conducted at the White House.

Lizzie understood the first lady better than anyone else. She was able to provide her with the emotional support Mrs. Lincoln required to cope with her tragedy.

CHAPTER EIGHT

As Union victories spread throughout the South, hundreds of thousands of frightened, bewildered, and homeless slaves flocked to Union lines, carrying with them their meager possessions. Because the law acknowledged them as possessions, the army justified accepting slaves by ranking them with abandoned rebel cattle and corn as contraband of war. So they became known as "contrabands." Several thousand made their way to the nation's capital. Streets and open spaces were already filled with tents, troops, supply wagons, ambulances, makeshift hospitals, and injured soldiers. Many contrabands mistakenly believed that the government would feed and clothe them, and that they would never be overworked again.

Lizzie often visited camps set up by the federal government called Freedmen's Villages. At "Murder Bay," the Freedmen camp situated between Thirteenth and Fifteenth streets and bordering the dank and smelly Washington Canal, entire families were crowded into small makeshift shanties. Filth and stagnant water seeped through the rough floorboards, and the roofs leaked when it rained. Airless and windowless rooms measuring only six or eight feet square were often entirely surrounded by other rooms.

Lizzie found men, women, and children huddled together. Many were sick with measles, diphtheria, scarlet

or typhoid fever. They lay on the bare dirt floor.

Slaves who had spent their lives working, living, and sleeping in open fields detested the crowded shanties that confined them. Knowing only the feel of farm tools, a cotton pod, and an overseer's whip, some of them had never sat at a dining table or used a knife and fork.

When Lizzie visited the village, crowds gathered about her. Dressed in fashionable elegance, she carried herself with poise and dignity, and the newly freed slaves looked to her for explanations and answers.

Two tattered contrabands. (COURTESY OF THE MASSACHUSETTS COMMANDERY MILITARY ORDER OF THE LOYAL LEGION AND THE U.S. ARMY MILITARY INSTITUTE.)

Dependence had become second nature to them. Many believed President and Mrs. Lincoln would care for their needs. One old woman who had spent her entire

Elizabeth Hobbs Keckley, daguerreotype by Nicholas H. Sheperd. (COURTESY OF THE LINCOLN MUSEUM, FORT WAYNE, INDIANA, A PART OF THE LINCOLN NATIONAL CORPORATION.)

Newly freed slaves. (COURTESY OF THE LIBRARY OF CONGRESS.)

life on a plantation seemed to represent the feelings of many others. She told Lizzie she had been in the camp for eight months and Mrs. Lincoln hadn't given her even one dress. If she had known that the government and Mr. and Mrs. Lincoln were going to be like that, she never would have left the plantation. Her old mistress had given her two "shifes" (dresses) a year. She felt that President and Mrs. Lincoln were very cruel for overlooking the custom. Lizzie often heard many of the former slaves say they'd rather go back to slavery in the South and be with their old masters than enjoy the freedom of the North. Many Northern abolitionists, when faced with the needs of the newly freed slaves, turned their backs on their plight or looked on them with indifference.

Lizzie followed the camp children's education through twelve of their teachers, good friends of hers, whose jobs she probably helped secure. They reported to her that the children learned to read quickly.

Lizzie organized sewing circles where she helped women make quilts, mend old donated clothing, and talk about what life in freedom was like. Slave women often expressed themselves through the quilts they made, depicting significant events of their lives in patterns of the piecework. The craft provided an outlet for them to talk about their hopes and aspirations while sitting about a quilting frame.

Lizzie was proud of those former slaves whose spirits had not been totally crushed and who used their freedom to build cabins and plant small vegetable gardens within the village. Some eventually owned a pig and a dozen or more chickens.

The problems and needs of the freed slaves were never far from Lizzie's thoughts. One warm summer evening when she and a friend took a stroll in her neighborhood, they heard the music of a live band and came upon a brightly lighted yard where well-dressed ladies and gentlemen stood about talking.

When Lizzie asked about the festivity from a guard on duty, he informed her that proceeds raised from the event would be donated to sick and wounded white soldiers.

This gave Lizzie an idea. She said to her friend, "If the white people can give festivals to raise funds for the relief of suffering soldiers, why shouldn't the well-to-do colored people go to work for the benefit of suffering blacks?"

The following Sunday she attended church and spoke before a black congregation. She suggested that black people form a society to benefit impoverished newly freed slaves. Forty people volunteered to be members, and the organization became known as the First Black Contraband Relief Organization. Members elected Lizzie as president.

The next month Lizzie accompanied Mrs. Lincoln on a shopping trip to New York, where they lodged at the Metropolitan Hotel. There Lizzie vividly described the sad conditions of the freed slaves. Touched by their plight, Mrs. Lincoln took immediate action.

In a letter Mrs. Lincoln wrote to the president from New York, she informed him: "These immense number of Contrabands [freed slaves] are suffering intensely, many without bedcovering and having to use any bits of carpeting to cover themselves—many dying of want. . . . Out of the $1,000 fund deposited with you by General [Michael] Corcoran, I have given [Keckley] the privilege of investing $200 here in bedcovering. . . . The cause of humanity requires it." The money the Lincolns donated came from a fund designated for white soldiers. Mrs. Lincoln also contributed fifteen boxes of clothing, five hundred tin plates, twenty turkeys, and several boxes of apples and cranberries.

Both Mrs. Lincoln and Lizzie raised funds for the First Black Contraband Relief Organization, though Mrs. Lincoln quickly discovered it was easier to raise money for white soldiers than for former black slaves.

After their trip to New York, Mrs. Lincoln invited Lizzie to accompany her to Boston, where she planned to visit her eldest son, Robert, at Harvard University.

Lizzie held a mass meeting at the Colored Baptist Church in Boston and, with the help of the minister, raised money and organized a branch of the First Black Contraband Relief Organization. They sent more than eighty boxes of clothing and other goods to the association's Washington headquarters and raised funds through admission fees to dramatic readings and speeches. Frederick Douglass, a former slave and good friend of Lizzie's, who became one of the greatest and most respected orators of the nineteenth century on rights of black people and of women, lectured on behalf of the society and contributed two hundred dollars.

Returning to New York, Lizzie approached the black steward at the Metropolitan Hotel, who immediately raised funds from among the dining room waiters. Black women in the city organized a ball to benefit the hapless, newly freed slaves.

Lizzie's organization spread to Philadelphia and then to England and Scotland. And Mrs. Lincoln and the president made frequent contributions.

In 1863 Lizzie was reelected president of the entire growing organization, a post she held until 1868, when the contrabands no longer needed that kind of assistance. In 1864 the association changed its name to the Freedmen and Soldiers' Relief Association of Washington. People who knew Lizzie reported that funds left from the association after it disbanded in 1868 were donated to the Home for Destitute Women and Children in Washington, D.C., where Lizzie would spend her final years.

CHAPTER NINE

ON NEW YEAR'S Day, 1863—the day President Lincoln signed the Emancipation Proclamation—the Lincolns opened the White House for a morning public reception for the first time since Willie's death. Lizzie dressed Mrs. Lincoln in a secondary mourning outfit of purple and white.

News of the Emancipation Proclamation reached every corner of the land, including the Confederate states. This historic document freed slaves in the rebellious states and permitted black men to join the army. Black people everywhere rejoiced. Black women wore wide-brimmed bonnets, lace shawls, fancy silk dresses with crinoline petticoats, and dainty shoes. Their finery symbolized that the slavery days of coarse tunics and bare feet were gone forever.

Lizzie's finances worried her. Orders for ball gowns had virtually ceased. In addition to her ongoing expenses, she had debts of two hundred dollars, she owed Wilberforce University one hundred dollars, the balance of her dead son's tuition, and she also needed to repay her former patrons in St. Louis the last hundred dollars of the twelve hundred dollars she had borrowed to buy freedom for herself and George.

A loyal friend and former St. Louis patron came to

One of several ornamental designs surrounding the Emancipation Proclamation issued in 1863. This one is embellished by a linked chain giving the names of all thirty-eight states and drawings suggesting public schools, commerce and free enterprise, freedom and mobility, recreation as well as work, united families, and religious freedom. (COURTESY OF THE LIBRARY OF CONGRESS.)

her aid. She visited to express sympathy over young George's death and to persuade Lizzie to apply for a government pension given to any woman who was a widow or mother of a dead soldier. To be eligible for the pension, Lizzie was required to state on the application that she and Alexander Kirkland had been married. Since they had not been married and Kirkland had never contributed to her and George's support or even acknowledged George as his son, Lizzie was very hesitant to apply for a pension. Kirkland had died when George was eighteen months old. Lizzie especially hated the thought of making money from her son's death. Her friend, however, overruled her objections, and soon Lizzie began to receive eight dollars a month. Eventually the monthly sum was increased to twelve dollars and became Lizzie's chief means of support in her old age.

To help supplement her income, and because she loved to surround herself with young people, Lizzie conducted sewing classes in her workrooms for young black girls. She draped assorted fabrics in a variety of styles on a wooden figure she used as a model. A wooden sign outside advertised her school.

Lizzie was an exacting teacher. She insisted that her students sit up straight at all times. She forbade them to sit leaning over while the work rested on their knees, a practice that caused rounded shoulders and hunched backs. She instructed her students to walk tall, talk with their heads held high, and to look people in the eye when speaking or being spoken to. She trained them in business matters and showed them, by her own example, her polished technique of dealing with patrons. Many future seamstresses would attribute their success to Lizzie.

Mrs. Lincoln saw an opportunity for Lizzie to earn additional income at the Treasury Department. For the first time in history, women were hired to take the places of men in offices, factories, and farms as the men left to become soldiers. Women were seen wearing long, cumbersome hooped skirts that swept unpaved streets as they reported for work in the nation's capital. The secretary of the treasury, Salmon P. Chase, ordered a walking board to be placed across muddy Pennsylvania Avenue to save them from sinking knee-deep in mud.

Mrs. Lincoln wrote a letter on March 20, 1863, to Mr. George Harrington, the assistant secretary of the treasury. She requested a job for Lizzie in the note-cutting room of the Treasury Department, where many seamstresses, skilled with scissors, cut paper currency from large printed sheets. Although Mrs. Lincoln had successfully secured jobs for many former slaves as clerks, watchmen, and lamplighters, she failed to move the Treasury Department to hire Lizzie. Records show black women were hired at the Treasury Department as office cleaners, or charwomen, not as female clerks paid six hundred dollars per year (a high salary in 1863, although the sum was half that paid to men). White women probably would have refused to work alongside a black woman.

Lizzie's devotion to Mrs. Lincoln proved limitless. On July 2, 1863, Mrs. Lincoln fell from her carriage when the coachman's seat became detached and he was thrown to the ground. As the uncontrolled horses galloped away, Mrs. Lincoln jumped from the moving vehicle. She sustained a severe head injury, which bled

Sojourner Truth presenting a Bible to President Lincoln. From Homespun Heroines & Other Women of Distinction, *circa 1926.* (USED BY PERMISSION OF MOORLAND-SPINGARN RESEARCH CENTER, HOWARD UNIVERSITY.)

profusely and then became infected. Lizzie took over when nurses were no longer needed to care for her.

While Lizzie tended Mrs. Lincoln, the war took a turn for the better. A three-day battle raged at Gettysburg, where Union troops defeated Confederate General Lee's northernmost army. At the same time, the city of Vicksburg fell; from this location Confederate troops had controlled traffic on the Mississippi River.

Because of Lizzie's access to the Lincolns, several people professed to be her friend and tried to reach them through her. Although she was often asked questions about the first family, she was careful not to say too much. She was also consulted on important matters by leaders of her people. She arranged appointments for them with Mr. Lincoln. One of these leaders was the former slave Sojourner Truth, an eloquent speaker on the rights of blacks and women, and a teacher of the freedmen and their children.

As reelection time drew near, Lizzie noticed that Mrs. Lincoln grew increasingly nervous. One morning the first lady confided that there was more at stake in this election than Mr. Lincoln ever dreamed of. Lizzie listened attentively as the first lady confessed that she owed twenty-seven thousand dollars to various stores, a debt her husband knew nothing about and would be unable to repay if he was defeated.

Because of her high station, and to tempt Mrs. Lincoln to buy more merchandise, many store clerks flattered her and extended her unlimited credit. They would demand payment if she no longer had power as the president's wife. The debt could be kept secret from her husband and from his enemies only if he was reelected, because then the merchants would continue to extend credit.

Mrs. Lincoln justified her actions to Lizzie: "You understand, Lizabeth [a name she sometimes called Lizzie], that Mr. Lincoln has but little idea of the expense of a woman's wardrobe. He glances at my rich dresses and is happy in the belief that the few hundred dollars that I obtain from him supply all my wants. I must dress in costly materials. The people scrutinize every article I wear. . . . To keep up appearances, I must have money—more than Mr. Lincoln can spare me. He is too honest to make a penny outside of his salary; consequently I had, and still have no alternative but to run into debt."

Lizzie understood Mrs. Lincoln's need to be the best dressed. The first lady believed her clothing proved she had culture and fine taste and deserved to be the wife of a president.

Mrs. Lincoln thought her expensive dresses might prove to be of financial help someday. She told Lizzie that she and Mr. Lincoln would probably leave the White House poorer than when they arrived and then she would sell her clothes.

Criticism of Mr. Lincoln grew daily. Many white men rebelled when they were drafted into the army and called upon to risk their lives to free the slaves. Draft riots erupted throughout the North. During the summer of 1863 a mob in New York City marched down Broadway, burned whole city blocks, smashed windows, knocked down telegraph poles, and destroyed a million dollars' worth of property. They beat to death and hanged dozens of Negroes and set fire to the Colored Orphan Asylum. The Visiting Committee of Lizzie's First Black Contraband Relief Organization distributed groceries and clothing to many homeless black people whose homes were destroyed in the riot. As the war raged on and the death toll rose, the press called Mr. Lincoln, among other things, an ape, a baboon, a clown, a usurper, a traitor, a monster, an idiot, a bigot, a lunatic, a despot, a blunderer, and a bully. One newspaper said he should be exhibited as a zoological curiosity. The *Illinois State Register* called him "the craftiest and most dishonest politician that ever disgraced an office in America."

When Mrs. Lincoln expressed concern over her husband's reelection, Lizzie reassured her that people of the North valued him and would surely reelect him. Her words soothed Mrs. Lincoln for a while.

Lizzie's steady acceptance of Mrs. Lincoln's unpredictable ways and her sympathetic understanding of Mrs. Lincoln's ever-present fear for her husband's safety helped to sustain the first lady. Mr. Lincoln received life-threatening letters almost daily. Lizzie said he never gave them a second thought, but they troubled Mrs. Lincoln severely. Unscreened strangers swarmed throughout the second-floor family quarters daily. Ward Hill Lamon, Mr. Lincoln's longtime friend who had accompanied him to Washington in 1861, slept on the floor outside Lincoln's bedroom armed with pistols and bowie knives. He said, "There was never a moment . . . that he was not in danger by violence."

William O. Stoddard, whose duty it was to screen

mail addressed to the Lincolns, remarked about Mrs. Lincoln: "It was not easy at first to understand why a lady could be one day so kindly, so considerate, so generous, so thoughtful and so hopeful, could upon another day appear so unreasonable, so irritable, so despondent, so even niggardly and so prone to see the dark, the wrong side of men and women and events."

Lizzie wrote that when Mrs. Lincoln was in one of her "wayward" impulsive moods, she tended to say and do things that wounded the president deeply. Lizzie felt sad whenever Mrs. Lincoln hurt her husband's feelings; she believed that the president loved his wife dearly and wanted nothing but affection from her.

Mrs. Lincoln had strong opinions about people who surrounded her husband. She viciously condemned members of his cabinet, generals, and women who fawned over him. Lizzie believed that in many cases the first lady's intuition about the sincerity of certain people was more accurate than the president's.

Mrs. Lincoln detested the secretary of the treasury, Salmon P. Chase, and his beautiful young daughter, Kate. She believed he was nothing more than a selfish politician who could not be trusted. She excluded him from social events whenever possible. She called General Ulysses Grant a butcher and said that "he . . . is not fit to head an army. He loses two men to the enemies' one." Lizzie often heard Mrs. Lincoln say that if Grant should ever be elected president, she would leave the country and remain absent during his term of office. When General Grant ran for president, Mrs. Lincoln left the country.

Mr. Lincoln remarked that if things were left up to his wife, he would have no cabinet or generals.

Lizzie was rarely surprised by anything Mrs. Lincoln did or said. However, the first lady scandalized most people with her loose tongue and shocked those she wrote letters to, defaming prominent people. Although she ordered that her letters be destroyed after they were read, many were not.

Mrs. Lincoln often behaved hypocritically. She surrounded herself with men of questionable character and behaved coquettishly. Yet she flew into jealous rages whenever her husband so much as spoke to an attractive woman. She felt she could easily lose her husband's affections. She disguised her pain and insecurity by being harsh, insensitive, and arrogant. When she decided to discontinue the president's custom of choosing a female partner in a promenade about the room during each White House reception, she explained to Lizzie, "I am his wife and I should lead with him. And yet he offers his arm to any other lady in the room, making her first with him and placing me second. The custom is an absurd one, and I mean to abolish it."

The president not only tolerated his wife's behavior but often acceded to her wishes. In this case the president either led the promenade with his wife, walked alone, or walked with a gentleman. Yet Mrs. Lincoln continued to choose a male partner. She was severely criticized for breaking the president's custom and continuing her own.

One day while Lizzie dressed Mrs. Lincoln and Mr. Lincoln was present, his wife objected to the women he might speak with at that evening's reception. Mr. Lincoln replied, "I can't stand around like a simpleton and say nothing. If you will not tell me who I may talk with, please tell me who I may not talk with."

Mrs. Lincoln named two women she hated and another who would flatter him. Mr. Lincoln replied, "Very well, mother; now that we have settled the question to your satisfaction, we will go down-stairs."

Mrs. Lincoln was severely criticized for her apparent insensitivity to the war effort. Mary Clemmer Ames, one of her foremost critics, wrote: "Wharves were lined with bodies of the dead. The rivers carried freight after freight of lacerated men. One ceaseless procession of ambulances moved to and fro. Churches, halls, and houses were turned into hospitals. Every railroad train that entered the city bore fresh troops—fresh mourners sought their dead. Throughout it all, Mrs. Lincoln shopped."

The unfairness of unjust criticism angered Lizzie. Lizzie was one of few people aware of the first lady's visits to hospitals throughout Washington. She carried flowers, donated gifts, and wrote letters for thousands of wounded men. She ordered delicacies delivered from the White House kitchens and stopped to buy special foods soldiers wanted or needed and paid for them herself. One of the hospitals was named after her.

Rumors circulated throughout Washington that Mrs. Lincoln spied for the Confederacy. It was said that rebels came by ladder to her bedroom window, where she passed military secrets to them. The *Cincinnati Commercial* stated that Mrs. Lincoln's Confederate relatives "were all secessionists and it was suspected that her sympathies were rather with the rebellion."

The first lady had three half brothers, one brother, and four brothers-in-law who all served in the Confederate army. One worked as a surgeon in a Confederate hospital, another died leading a charge at the Battle of Shiloh in

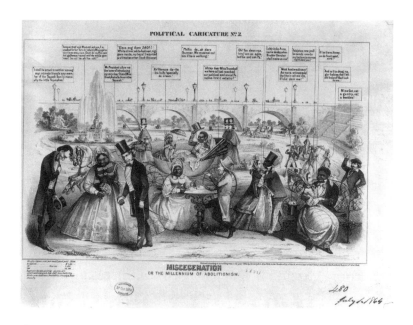

Caricature on miscegenation mocking Mrs. Lincoln's friendship with Lizzie and forecasting the nature of future relationships between black and white people. Printed by the publisher Bromley & Company in 1864. (COURTESY OF THE LIBRARY OF CONGRESS.)

1862, and another was the commander of a prisoner-of-war camp who treated prisoners so cruelly and brutally that Jefferson Davis removed him from his post. Mary Lincoln hadn't seen or spoken with those members of her family for years. Besides, she told Lizzie, she could neither mourn nor feel sympathy for Confederate members of her family who, if they could, would hang her husband and perhaps her as well.

The Committee on the Conduct of War convened in secret session in early 1863 to consider rumors of Mrs. Lincoln's treason. When President Lincoln appeared, unsummoned, hat in hand, and stood at the end of their long table and swore no member of his family spied for the Confederacy, the committee dropped the investigation.

Lizzie's relationship with Mrs. Lincoln attracted the poison pen of the press. Many people—even several abolitionists—disapproved of Mary Lincoln's selection of a black woman as her best friend. A cartoon appeared in the newspaper that depicted their friendship as beginning a trend of miscegenation (interbreeding, especially marriage between two races).

Toward the end of the summer of 1864, Mrs. Lincoln traveled to Lizzie's rooms, presumably to discuss a dress, but really to readdress her concerns about Mr. Lincoln's reelection. Lizzie once again reassured her and said, "I am so confident of it [his reelection], that I am tempted to ask a favor." Lizzie wanted the white kid glove Mr. Lincoln would wear on his right hand to shake the hands of thousands of people at the first White House reception after his second inauguration. Mrs. Lincoln said Lizzie was welcome to the glove but that it would be so filthy after he shook so many hands, she would be tempted to hold it with tongs and throw it into the fire. She could not imagine why Lizzie would want such a glove.

Lizzie explained, "I shall cherish it as a precious memento of the second inauguration of a man who has done so much for my race. He . . . has lifted them [the black people] out of bondage, and directed their footsteps from darkness into light. I shall keep the glove, and hand it down to posterity."

Mrs. Lincoln commented that Lizzie had some strange ideas; nevertheless, she could have the glove if Mr. Lincoln was reelected.

CHAPTER TEN

IN 1864 GENERAL William Tecumseh Sherman and his troops had swept across Tennessee, through Georgia, and on to the Carolinas. His men cut down forests and burned homes, barns, fields, killed livestock, and tore up railroad tracks. They leveled a forty-mile-wide path through the heart of the Confederacy, severing it into two parts. The South was no longer able to wage an effective war. Sherman's success helped President Lincoln become reelected.

The Lincolns were severely criticized because their eldest son, Robert, did not serve in the military. Lizzie would share the real story four years later in the book she wrote.

Robert returned to the White House every few months from Harvard, eager to quit school and serve in the army. Mrs. Lincoln refused to hear of it. She would say, "We have lost one son, and his loss is as much as I can bear without being called upon to make another sacrifice."

Mr. Lincoln would answer, "But many a poor mother has given up all her sons . . . our son is not more dear to us than the sons of other people are to their mothers. . . . The services of every man who loves his country are required in this war. You should take a liberal instead of a selfish view of the question, Mother."

President Lincoln's second inauguration in front of the Capitol, March 4, 1865. Wood engraving in Frank Leslie's Illustrated Newspaper, *March 18, 1865.* (COURTESY OF THE LIBRARY OF CONGRESS.)

Mrs. Lincoln finally relented, and on February 11, 1865, two months before the war would end, Robert joined General Grant's staff as a captain.

Thousands of people gathered in Washington for the festivities of Lincoln's second inauguration on March 4, 1865. Walt Whitman, a noted poet who lived in the nation's capital, described the day as miserable, with raging winds and rain that uprooted trees. The *Evening Star* reported that police were insisting that all pedestrians who could not swim be confined to the sidewalks.

Lizzie went to the White House to dress Mrs. Lincoln for the first grand levee of Mr. Lincoln's second term in office. While Lizzie brushed Mrs. Lincoln's hair, President Lincoln entered the room. It was the first time Lizzie had seen him after his inaugural speech. She crossed the room, extended her hand, and congratulated him. He grasped her hand warmly. Lizzie felt humble as the hand that freed three and a half million of her brethren held hers. "Well, Madam Eliz," Lincoln said to her, "I don't know whether I should feel thankful or not. The position brings with it many trials. We do not know what we are destined to pass thru."

He gently dropped her hand, walked across the room, sat on a sofa, lifted a Bible, and soon became absorbed in reading.

When Lizzie had congratulated Mrs. Lincoln earlier, the first lady had sighed deeply and said now that they had won the position, she almost wished it were otherwise. Her husband was so completely worn out and heartbroken, she feared he wouldn't get through the next four years.

Lizzie finished dressing Mrs. Lincoln, who took her husband's arm and walked downstairs into one of the largest receptions ever held in Washington. Every available space was packed with people. District police managed people inside, and the military managed those outside. Occasionally a woman would faint and have to be rescued; her body would be passed over the heads of people jammed so closely, no one could move. Over six thousand people shook President Lincoln's hand wearing one of the gloves that Lizzie would own.

Grand White House reception, 1865. (COURTESY OF THE LIBRARY OF CONGRESS.)

A congressman spotted Frederick Douglass on the outskirts of the crowd waiting outside the White House to shake the president's hand. He escorted the former slave and renowned orator to Mr. Lincoln, who greeted him warmly. Frederick Douglass then attended one of the parties where Lizzie was a guest and informed her of his encounter with the president.

For the Inaugural Ball commemorating his second term in office, held two days later, Lizzie spent most of the day with Mrs. Lincoln and dressed her in an elegant white satin gown with an overlay of white point lace with puffs of silk. Mrs. Lincoln carried a fan of ermine and silver spangles and wore white gloves, a pearl necklace, and earrings. Her hair was swept back into curls, and a wreath of intertwined white jasmine and purple violets crowned her head.

Lizzie had no way of knowing at the time that the Inaugural Ball would be the last time President and Mrs. Lincoln would appear formally together in public and that the ball gown would be the last festive dress Mrs. Lincoln would wear.

CHAPTER ELEVEN

THE WAR WAS drawing to an end. Telegraph wires continued to carry good news every day about Northern victories.

On March 23 President and Mrs. Lincoln left Washington to visit City Point, the command and supply center for General Grant's troops. From City Point they sailed up the James River to Malvern Hill on General Grant's steamship, the *Mary Martin*, to review the troops of General E. O. C. Ord. Before the review, they had lunch aboard the flagship *Malvern*. After lunch the party went ashore and President Lincoln, astride General Grant's fast Kentucky Thoroughbred, Cincinnati, a horse that had ridden through the fiercest battles of the Civil War, rode ahead, escorted by General Ord and many other officers. Mary Lincoln and Julia Grant, General Grant's wife, along with two colonels as escorts, followed the procession in an ambulance. Mrs. Mary Ord, General Ord's wife, intended to ride in the ambulance with the two women but found there was no room. An accomplished equestrian, she mounted a horse and, along with her assigned escort for the day, rode behind President Lincoln's cavalcade. The small half-open ambulance carrying Mrs. Lincoln and Mrs. Grant fell behind on the two-mile trip, hampered by the muddy road with its grooves from wagon wheels. Mrs. Lincoln asked the driver to speed up, but President Lincoln had begun his

General E. O. C. Ord and his wife, Mary Ord, with their daughter on the porch of the Confederate executive mansion in 1865. (COURTESY OF THE MASSACHUSETTS COMMANDERY MILITARY ORDER OF THE LOYAL LEGION AND THE U.S. ARMY MILITARY HISTORY INSTITUTE.)

review of the troops before his wife's arrival because he was running late and the soldiers had not yet eaten lunch. No other visitors were present, and Mrs. Ord, feeling awkward about having no official position on the parade ground, asked an army officer if it would be proper for her to join the review. When he answered, "Of course!" she rode up to join Mr. Lincoln. Minutes later when the ambulance carrying Mrs. Lincoln and Mrs. Grant rolled into view, Mrs. Lincoln became so enraged at the sight of Mrs. Ord riding next to Mr. Lincoln that Mrs. Grant feared the first lady would leap from the vehicle. Mrs. Grant attempted to calm her by defending Mrs. Ord. Mrs. Lincoln turned her wrath upon Mrs. Grant, accusing her of wanting to be the first lady.

When Mrs. Ord spied the ambulance, she and her escort galloped across the field to join the ladies. An eyewitness, Adam Badeau, described the scene. Mrs. Lincoln called Mrs. Ord vile names within earshot of a crowd of officers and asked what she meant by following the president. Mrs. Ord broke into tears and had to be helped away.

From that day on, Mrs. Lincoln and Mrs. Grant were enemies, and Mrs. Lincoln secluded herself on the *River Queen* steamer for five days. President Lincoln believed the pressure and excitement of being so close to the front had proved too severe for his wife's unsteady nerves. He suggested she return to the capital, and she did.

It was Monday, April 3, 1865, that Mrs. James Harlan, Robert Lincoln's future mother-in-law, visited Lizzie's boardinghouse rooms for a fitting of a dress she had ordered. Lizzie noticed men and artillery pass by her window on their way to open ground to fire a salute in honor of another Northern victory.

Lizzie leaned from her window and asked one of the soldiers the reason for the celebration. He gleefully shouted that Richmond, the capital of the Confederacy, had fallen. Mrs. Harlan grabbed both of Lizzie's hands and the two women laughed, hugged, and whirled around the room in joy.

Lizzie excused herself and ran across the street to her workshop. Her employees had heard the news and were dancing about with excitement. The victory was especially joyful because they had heard that the Thirty-sixth U.S. Colored Troops had been the first regiment to enter and occupy the Confederate capital. The long-awaited victory meant that the end of the four-year struggle was near.

Lizzie's workers reminded her of the promise she had made months before to declare a holiday when Richmond fell. Now Lizzie felt torn. Mrs. Harlan needed her work done quickly, and Lizzie's philosophy was always work before pleasure.

Returning to her rooms, Lizzie offered Mrs. Harlan the choice of having her work completed on time or a postponement while she and her workers celebrated. Mrs. Harlan said she would gladly wait and that, by all means, Lizzie should give her staff a holiday.

Lizzie linked arms with her employees and wandered about the city, singing and clapping along with the rest of the populace. Government workers poured from public buildings and joined the merriment. Even courts recessed for the day. Some people waved flags from balconies, others waved handkerchiefs from windows, some made speeches, and bands played "Yankee Doodle."

Mrs. Lincoln felt remorseful over her angry departure from her husband and Tad, soon to celebrate his twelfth birthday, who had remained with General Grant. She decided to rejoin them, and she invited Lizzie to accompany her and other guests on her return to City Point and her tour of the fallen Southern capital. The group included Senator Charles Sumner, Mrs. Harlan and her daughter, Robert Lincoln's future wife, a young French nobleman, Attorney General James Speed, and Judge William Otto, secretary of the interior.

Lizzie was delighted. Richmond and City Point were near the city of Petersburg, where she had often visited when she lived in Dinwiddie Courthouse with the Garlands.

Lizzie and the first lady's party boarded the steamer U.S.S. *Monohassett* at 11:00 A.M. on April 5, 1865, and sailed down the polluted Potomac River. When they reached the James River, which had been cleared of battle debris, dead horses, crates and boxes, the air became fresh and pure. Lizzie stood on the upper deck and breathed deeply. The fields along the river had changed considerably since she had last seen them. Deserted camps, half-standing forts, scattered weapons, and abandoned broken cannons dotted war-ravaged fields where the blood of brothers who had fought brothers soaked the earth.

The steamer docked at City Point, and the party boarded the *River Queen* where President Lincoln briefed

Remains of Richmond after Confederate troops burned the city in 1865. (COURTESY OF THE LIBRARY OF CONGRESS.)

them on troop movements. He arranged for the *River Queen* to sail them to Richmond that afternoon.

Destruction greeted Lizzie's eyes as she toured the fallen Confederate capital. Before the rebel troops had retreated, they had set fire to the city. The dense air, filled with debris from smoldering business buildings and homes, made breathing difficult.

Lizzie walked to the former Confederate headquarters, the capitol building, one of the few buildings spared the torch. She stepped carefully between broken desks and overturned chairs. Among papers scattered about the floor, she picked up a resolution prohibiting all free black people from entering the state of Virginia. She walked into the senate chamber, and when she sat in Jefferson Davis's chair, she could not help remembering Christmas Eve four years earlier when she had put the finishing touches on his robe. So much had happened since then.

Leaving the capitol building, Lizzie rejoined Mrs. Lincoln's party as they visited the Davis family home that had served as the Confederate White House, now used as Union general Godfrey Weitzel's headquarters. Lizzie was curious to see their Southern residence. Their home in Washington had been so familiar to her when she made daily visits there to sew for Mrs. Davis.

Lizzie climbed the stairs from the ground floor to the family's living quarters on the floor above. The sideboard, dining table, gold-framed mirror over the fireplace, and a bust of Confederate General Stonewall Jackson stood in the dining room. Surprisingly, the green-and-white Brussels carpeting with matching drapes had been spared. Most rugs throughout the South had been used to make carpet slippers. Draperies had been made into clothing. Rumor had it that Mrs. Davis had cut apart her wedding gown to make clothes for her children.

As Lizzie walked up the circular staircase to the master bedroom and nursery, she felt the personal tragedy that had struck the Davis family. Their five-year-old son had fallen to his death the year before from an outside

*P*resident Lincoln visits the Confederate White House in Richmond, Virginia, April 4, 1865. From a sketch by artist Joseph Becker. (COURTESY OF THE LIBRARY OF CONGRESS.)

porch attached to their bedroom. When she left the house, she was acutely aware of the many changes the years had brought. She wrote, "I, who was once a slave, . . . punished with the cruel lash . . . experienced the . . . torture of a slave's life, can say to Mr. Jefferson Davis, 'Peace! You have suffered! Go in peace.' "

That night, the *River Queen* was docked at City Point. In the steamer's cabin everyone appeared happy until a young officer seated next to Mrs. Lincoln described how young ladies had blown kisses and waved handkerchiefs at her husband when he first en-

Jefferson Davis, former senator from Mississippi and president of the Confederacy. (COURTESY OF THE MASSACHUSETTS COMMANDERY MILITARY ORDER OF THE LOYAL LEGION AND THE U.S. ARMY MILITARY HISTORY INSTITUTE.)

tered Richmond. Mrs. Lincoln became so incensed over the young man's remark that she demanded he be put off the ship. This incident was just one more example of the first lady's irrational behavior.

Although Lizzie's loyalty to Mrs. Lincoln was unquestionable, the first lady's behavior often caused Lizzie to say, "I never saw a more peculiarly constituted woman. Search the world over, and you will not find her counterpart."

The next day Lizzie boarded a train with the presidential party for Petersburg, Virginia. Several black waiters from the *River Queen* joined them, and the waiters and Lizzie sat in the same car with the Lincolns.

Lizzie wandered off by herself in Petersburg searching for people she had known in former days. Mostly everyone she encountered was a stranger, and the few people she did recognize revived painful memories.

Lizzie gladly left Petersburg and boarded the train to return to City Point. The trip was made especially pleasant when the president spied a terrapin on a rock basking in the sun. He asked the conductor to stop the train and bring the turtle on board. Lizzie enjoyed watching the delight of Tad and Mr. Lincoln as they amused themselves with the animal's clumsy antics for the remainder of the trip.

The *River Queen* remained docked for a few days. Although Mrs. Lincoln's behavior sometimes caused her husband anguish, Lizzie had never seen him so relaxed. He lounged on the boat, left occasionally for excursions, and talked with everyone who came on board.

On their last evening, the vessel looked like an enchanted floating palace with multicolored kerosene lamps sparkling in the twilight. A military band played while several Union officers came aboard to say farewell. Mrs. Lincoln was still angry with General Grant's wife for defending Mrs. Ord's riding next to Mr. Lincoln in the review of troops. The first lady refused to invite General and Mrs. Grant to the farewell party. The general and his wife threw a party of their own on their boat with live music and sailed alongside the docked *River Queen* competing with the merriment on the president's boat.

Lizzie vividly remembered that night. When the president had been asked to make a speech, he said he was too tired, but he promised to deliver one the following Tuesday in Washington. Then he asked the band to play "Dixie," the popular Confederate song, and remarked, "It has always been a favorite of mine, and since we have captured it, we have a perfect right to enjoy it."

At 11:00 P.M. the lights were taken down, and the

River Queen left the dock, churning the waters en route to Washington. Upon arriving there the next evening, Sunday, April 9, Lizzie and the other members of the traveling party went their separate ways. President Lincoln learned from Edwin M. Stanton, the secretary of war, that Lee's army had surrendered to Union forces at Appomattox Courthouse that afternoon. The war had finally come to an end!

CHAPTER TWELVE

ON MONDAY, APRIL 10, the day after Lee's surrender, cannons boomed, guns fired salutes, bands played, people sang and cheered. Government buildings and businesses closed to commemorate the war's end. Lizzie asked Mrs. Lincoln if she and a friend might attend Mr. Lincoln's speech the next night. In the four years she had been with the Lincolns, Lizzie had never attended any White House function as a guest. She had always remained behind the scenes in the family quarters.

"Certainly," Mrs. Lincoln answered, and asked that she be on time to dress her before the event.

Lizzie arrived at the White House about seven o'clock. While passing the president's office, she saw his lips move silently as he read over his notes.

As Lizzie walked down the hall to the first lady's quarters, she wondered why she was so nervous about being a guest at a White House function. After she dressed Mrs. Lincoln, Lizzie walked down the hall to a large second-floor window that overlooked a large crowd below, which had gathered to hear Mr. Lincoln speak. Soon Mr. Lincoln appeared, and when he stepped from the window onto a connecting balcony over the front door of the White House, the Marine Band stopped playing and the crowd burst into thunderous applause.

Lizzie stood a short distance behind the president. In her book she described the scene: "The swaying motion of the crowd, in the dim uncertain light, was like . . . the ebb and flow of the tide upon the stranded shore of the ocean. It was a grand and imposing scene, and when the President . . . advanced to speak, he looked more like a demi-god than a man."

A gas lamp was brought so he could read his notes. Twelve-year-old Tad rushed to his father's side and shouted, "Let me hold the light, Papa! Let me hold the light!" As Tad held the lamp, he looked up with pride and admiration at his father. It was a special moment that Lizzie always remembered.

The light from the lamp made the president stand out boldly in the darkness. A terrifying thought struck Lizzie, and she whispered to her friend, "What an easy matter it would be to kill the president! . . . He could be shot down from the crowd, and no one would be able to tell who fired the shot."

Lizzie said later, "I do not know what put such an idea into my head unless it was the sudden remembrance of the many warnings Mr. Lincoln had received."

When Lizzie mentioned her own strange and upsetting thought to Mrs. Lincoln, the president's wife sighed, "Yes, yes, Mr. Lincoln's life is always exposed. Ah, no one knows what it is [like] to live in constant dread of some fearful tragedy. The President has been warned so often that I tremble for him on every public occasion."

Mrs. Lincoln confided to Lizzie that she had had a premonition that the president would meet with a sudden and violent end. She said, "I pray God to protect my beloved husband from the hands of the assassin."

Only later would they discover that five conspirators

in his assassination plot had stood beneath the balcony that night.

Three days later, on April 14, 1865, General Robert Anderson, who had been forced to lower the Union flag at Fort Sumter exactly four years before, hoisted it there again in triumph. From the Atlantic to the Pacific, cities glowed with lights and flew flags and banners in celebration of the victories.

Lizzie saw Mrs. Lincoln for a few moments on April 14. Mrs. Lincoln told her she would not need her help getting dressed that night. She and the president planned a casual evening at Ford's Theatre to be followed by a late-night supper at the White House. While the Lincolns attended Ford's Theatre, crowds of people celebrating the Northern victories carried flaming torches as they marched down Pennsylvania Avenue. Flags flew from every window. Colorfully decorated lanterns swayed on ropes along buildings.

Lizzie went to bed early that night. The excitement and celebrations of the past few days had exhausted her. At about eleven o'clock, she was abruptly awoken by one of her neighbors, whose voice shook with incredulous disbelief as she frantically told her that Mr. Lincoln's entire cabinet had been assassinated and that Mr. Lincoln had been shot but not mortally wounded. In truth only Mr. William H. Seward of Mr. Lincoln's cabinet had been stabbed, and Mr. Lincoln would live only until the next morning.

Lizzie could barely catch her breath. She awoke the Lewises, the owners of her boardinghouse, and asked their help in getting to the White House. She knew Mrs. Lincoln needed her.

They dressed quickly and rushed into the street with Lizzie between them. The streets were filled with bewildered people. The Lewises and Lizzie were swept into the moving crowd, pushed and jostled toward the White House.

Every entrance to the presidential mansion was guarded by soldiers who permitted no one to pass. The guard at the gate where Lizzie had crossed hundreds of times before informed her that neither the president nor his wife had come to the White House. He refused to answer any further questions.

By the time they returned to the boardinghouse, Lizzie and the Lewises learned that Mr. Lincoln was not expected to live through the night.

Lizzie lay awake all night. The hours dragged while she envisioned Mrs. Lincoln wild with grief. Morning dawned cold, cheerless, and damp. Church bells tolled. President Lincoln was dead. Flags that had flown so proudly just hours before were now draped in black and hung at half-mast. People wandered the streets aimlessly.

Just before noon a messenger came by carriage to Lizzie's boardinghouse and asked her immediately to accompany him to the White House. Lizzie threw on her shawl and grabbed her bonnet.

She found Mrs. Lincoln writhing in bed, sobbing hysterically in her darkened bedroom. Mary Jane Welles, wife of Gideon Welles, one of the few Cabinet members Mrs. Lincoln did not dislike, had spent the night and was clearly relieved to see Lizzie. Lizzie massaged Mrs. Lincoln's temples and put cold compresses on her forehead.

The night before, at the William Petersen house,

where two doctors and other members of the audience had taken Mr. Lincoln from Ford's Theatre, Mrs. Welles had asked Mrs. Lincoln if there was anyone she would like to have with her. She had answered, "Lizzie Keckley." Three messengers were immediately sent to Lizzie's home, but in all the excitement they had copied down the wrong address.

Lizzie trembled as she entered the Guest Room, where the body of President Lincoln lay. Members of his cabinet and other officers of government stood around the body. As she moved closer, they stepped aside to make room for her. She could not help but recall the day the Lincolns' young son, little Willie, lay in his coffin exactly where the body of his father now rested.

She said, "I remembered how the President wept over the pale beautiful face of his gifted boy, and now the President himself was dead."

Lizzie lifted the cloth from the president's face. "There was something beautiful," she later wrote. "There lurked the sweetness and gentleness of childhood. . . . No common mortal had died. The Moses of my people had fallen . . . the brow was cold and pale in death." Tears choked her as she turned away.

Lizzie snipped several strands of Lincoln's bristly black hair that she had brushed and combed so often. Most likely she placed them next to Willie's golden locks that she had snipped after his death to wear in a locket or pin over her heart. Saving hair of a dead loved one and wearing it as jewelry was a popular custom of the time.

While Lizzie cared for Mrs. Lincoln on the second floor, some 30,000 mourners passed through the East

Room of the White House to pay their last respects to the assassinated president. People spoke in whispers and tiptoed about. They exited through a platform that had hastily been built through one of the windows.

After three days, the president's body was removed to the Rotunda of the Capitol, where it lay in state beneath the gigantic Statue of Freedom that had been completed during the war.

Within two weeks the conspirators in the assassination plot were arrested, and the president's assassin, John Wilkes Booth, had been tracked to a barn, cornered, and killed.

One night as Lizzie lay on a couch near Mrs. Lincoln's bed, the widow discovered that the guard on duty outside her room in the now vacant White House was the same one who had been on duty at Ford's Theatre the night her husband was killed. She ordered Lizzie to bring him to her.

While the guard stood before her, Mrs. Lincoln lashed out, "So you are on guard tonight—on guard in the White House after helping to murder the President."

The trembling guard stammered, "Pardon me, but I did not help to murder the President. . . . I could never stoop to murder—much less to the murder of so good and great a man as the President."

When Mrs. Lincoln said she did not believe him, he said, "I did wrong, I admit, and have bitterly repented. . . . I did not believe any one would try to kill so good a man in such a public place, and the belief made me careless. I was attracted by the play, and did not see the assassin enter the box."

Mrs. Lincoln told him he had no business to be careless and that she would always believe he was guilty. When he tried to answer, she told him to be quiet. With a wave of her hand, she motioned for him to leave the room. Mrs. Lincoln fell back upon her pillow, covered her face with her hands, and began to sob.

Lizzie helped the Lincolns' eldest son, Robert, pack sixty-four trunks and more than a hundred boxes in preparation for their move from the White House to Chicago, where Mrs. Lincoln decided to live. Mrs. Lincoln wanted to go someplace where she did not know anyone. She believed the sight of old friends and relatives would bring bad memories.

Many boxes were loosely packed with articles barely worth carrying away, such as outdated bonnets Mrs. Lincoln had brought from Springfield four years before. Others contained thousands of presents she and her children had received during Mr. Lincoln's presidency.

Once, as an old dress was being packed, Robert asked what his mother intended to do with it. When she answered she would find a use for it, her son blurted out, "I wish to heaven the car would take fire in which you place these boxes for transportation to Chicago, and burn all your plunder up."

Although Mrs. Lincoln refused to part with her old things, she gave away everything intimately connected with Mr. Lincoln, just as she had done with Willie's things after he died. Each item passed through Lizzie's hands. She gave Lizzie her cloak stained with the president's blood, along with a matching bonnet, the president's comb and brush, which Lizzie had used so often on his hair, his overshoes, and his gold watch.

The only article of furniture Mrs. Lincoln removed

from the White House was a small dressing stand Mr. Lincoln often used. Lizzie recalled the day he had stood before it and said, "Mother, this little stand is so handy and suits me so well that I do not know how I shall get along without it when we move away from here."

And his wife had replied that if he liked it that much, they should take it with them when they left the White House. When her husband objected, she suggested they replace it with a better one. And only then did Mr. Lincoln agree.

Mrs. Lincoln remembered their conversation and had the stand packed. The small piece of furniture would mean a lot to young Tad.

Mrs. Lincoln and Lizzie remained in the vacant White House for five weeks while newly sworn in President Andrew Johnson lived at the Kirkwood House, a hotel of sorts, and conducted the nation's business from the second floor of the Post Office. The security staff that usually guarded the executive mansion now guarded the new president. All day and all night, visitors, tourists, and collectors wandered through the unguarded first floor of the White House. With scissors and knives, they snipped pieces of carpet, lace curtains, and velvet wallpaper. They ripped upholstery from furniture and carried off silver and china. They spit tobacco juice everywhere while insects crawled over what furniture was left.

During their last week at the White House, Mrs. Lincoln lamented to Lizzie: "God, Elizabeth, what a change! Did ever a woman have to suffer so much and experience so great a change? I had ambition to be Mrs. President; that ambition has been gratified, and now I must step down from the pedestal. My poor husband! Had he never been President, he might be living today. Alas! All is over with me!"

May 22, 1865, the day to leave the executive mansion finally came. Lizzie said, "I can never forget that day; it was so unlike the day . . . the body of the President was born from the hall in grand and solemn state. . . . The silence was almost painful."

Barely anyone came to say good-bye. Crowds of people from different states had gathered in the nation's capital. Stands were being erected to seat thousands who arrived to witness the next day's grand review of Union troops by President Johnson and General Grant. All signs of mourning had been replaced by banners and flags celebrating final ceremonies before the troops returned home.

At about five o'clock, Mrs. Lincoln, Robert, Tad, and Lizzie walked down the public stairway, entered a horse-drawn carriage driven by the husband of Rosetta Wells, one of the women in the White House who had mended linens and torn clothing. Dr. Anson Henry, Mrs. Lincoln's friend and personal physician, and two White House guards joined them in a green railroad car that had been chartered for their use.

Mrs. Lincoln had a severe headache, and Lizzie bathed her temples for most of the night. Mrs. Lincoln said to her, "Lizabeth, you are my best and kindest friend, and I love you as my best friend. I wish it were in my power to make you comfortable for the balance of your days. If Congress provides for me, depend upon it, I will provide for you."

When Mrs. Lincoln had first asked Lizzie to accompany her to Chicago, Lizzie had refused adamantly. She had orders to fill for bridal trousseaus and fall outfits that were already behind schedule. She had not left Mrs. Lincoln's side for weeks. Mrs. Lincoln's mourning attire was purchased at Harper and Mitchell's Dry Goods Store. Government funds paid Lizzie thirty-five dollars a week for her services during Mrs. Lincoln's bereavement, one hundred dollars for travel expenses, her lodging in Chicago, and her return trip, and fifty dollars for Lizzie's mourning clothing. The sums the government paid were considerably smaller than Lizzie would have earned in her business.

Out of a sense of loyalty and pity, because Mrs. Lincoln desperately needed her, Lizzie closed her business.

As the fifty-four-hour train trip carried them closer to Chicago, Lizzie knew that a chapter in her life was closing and that another was about to begin.

CHAPTER THIRTEEN

CARRIAGES, CARTS, WAGONS, pedestrians, and soldiers crowded Chicago's narrow cobblestoned streets. Home from the war, many soldiers limped or used crutches. Others tried to hide an empty sleeve. Newspapers reported that Lincoln's assassin, John Wilkes Booth, had been secretly buried and that the other five conspirators had been sentenced to hang. The city's newspapers that had formerly carried every tidbit of gossip concerning Mrs. Lincoln were strangely silent now that she and her sons had moved there. No one welcomed or greeted her.

Mary Lincoln stayed in her hotel room their first week in the Windy City. Then she decided to move to three rooms in a less expensive rooming house in the newly opened summer resort of Hyde Park. Lizzie accompanied them and helped Robert unpack. She did not like Robert in the same way she liked the other Lincoln sons. She found him snobbish and distant. As they finished unpacking, he folded his arms, stood at one end of the fireplace, and asked Lizzie what she thought of their new quarters.

Lizzie answered, "This is a delightful place, and I think you will pass your time pleasantly."

Bitterness filled his voice as he answered. "You could feel that way because you don't have to live in them." With a note of desperation, he added, "I presume I must put up with it, as mother's pleasure must be consulted before my own."

Lizzie could understand his feelings about pleasing his mother, but not about the rooms. To her, they were lovely. Her years of slavery and deprivation had helped her to find beauty and joy in small things. She did not need grand rooms and great wealth to be happy.

Before she left Robert's room, he said, "I would almost as soon be dead as be compelled to remain three months in this dreary house."

Lizzie walked into Mrs. Lincoln's room and found her in bed sobbing. "What a dreary place, Lizzie!" she said. "And to think that I should be compelled to live here because I have not the means to live elsewhere. What a sad change has come to us all."

While Lizzie remained in Chicago with the Lincolns, the city hosted its second Sanitary Commission Fair. Sanitary Commissions were charitable organizations that raised funds for Union soldiers through fairs held in Northern cities. Proceeds from the events were donated to impoverished families of dead or injured Union soldiers.

President Lincoln had contributed the original draft of the Emancipation Proclamation document to the first Chicago Sanitary Commission Fair. It sold for three thousand dollars. On June 6, 1865, Lizzie visited the building where President Lincoln's catafalque, a tall domed canopy festooned with black silk, lined in white, lay covered within a glass dome. At its base lay relics of slavery from Southern plantations: a mammoth ball and chain by which slaves were bound, a variety of whips, and a score of other instruments of slave torture.

On the opposite side of the hall, for twenty-five cents, fairgoers could see a wax figure of Jefferson Davis dressed in a calico wraparound dress. The display attracted large crowds. Rumor had it that he was disguised as a woman when he was captured.

When Lizzie saw the figure, she instantly recognized the dress as one of the two chintzes she had made for Mrs. Davis when she sewed for her in Washington before the family had left for the South. Although usually reserved in her manner, Lizzie was so taken aback that she blurted out that she was the seamstress who had made that dress. The crowd standing near her became very excited and asked her to swear before a notary public that she had made it. The fair's chairwoman found a notary, and people gazed in awe as Lizzie swore.

The *Evening Journal* reported Lizzie's oath the next day, June 7, 1865:

> I hereby certify that I, Elizabeth Keckley, was originally dress-maker for Mrs. Jefferson Davis, that I have recently been dress-maker for Mrs. President Lincoln and have attended her from Washington to Chicago; that I have seen the figure of Jefferson Davis now on exhibition at Trophy Hall, and recognize the dress upon said figure as made by me for Mrs. Jefferson Davis, and worn by her.
>
> Elizabeth Keckley
>
> Chicago, June 6, 1865
> Witnesses: F. P. Fisher, Mrs. C. A. Lamb,
> Mrs. J. B. Bradwell

The certificate signed by Lizzie was pasted on the display. Ten thousand people spent twenty-five hundred dollars on lottery tickets for a chance to win the chintz wrapper on the Davis figure.

Lizzie planned to return to Washington after she had helped the Lincolns get settled in their new quarters. Mrs. Lincoln wanted her to stay but could not pay her expenses, and Lizzie could not afford to pay them herself.

Congress had allotted Mrs. Lincoln the first year's remainder of her husband's twenty-five-thousand-dollar salary for his second term (his four-year salary would have been $100,000) and seventeen hundred dollars a year until her death, the usual pension for a president's widow. Mrs. Lincoln's bills totaled seventy thousand dollars, a sum that overwhelmed her. She hired her children's former tutor to return merchandise, fend off creditors, stop the gossip about her extravagances, and solicit rich Republicans for donations. She petitioned Congress through letters and friends to increase her income by paying her the interest on what would have been her husband's remaining three-year salary. Congress denied her repeated requests.

Lizzie returned to Washington exhausted. She rested a few days, then visited former patrons, who were surprised to see her. They had expected her to spend the summer with Mrs. Lincoln. When Lizzie informed them that Mrs. Lincoln was poor, they seemed shocked. Newspapers reported that President Lincoln had left a sizable estate of more than one hundred thousand dollars. They did not know about Mrs. Lincoln's huge debt. Lizzie convinced everyone who inquired about the former first lady that she was poor and had to carefully budget every penny.

Lizzie rounded up her assistants, and orders began to come in more rapidly than she could fill them.

Soon after Lizzie's return from Chicago, a plain-looking woman with a black attendant arrived in an open carriage at Lizzie's workrooms. She asked if Lizzie would make one dress for her now, and several others, weeks later. Although Lizzie was unable to complete even one dress in less than three weeks, the woman accepted her terms.

Lizzie liked the woman's plain way of speaking and her direct manner. Before her newest patron left, Lizzie was dumbfounded when she introduced herself. "I am Mrs. Patterson [Martha Johnson], daughter of President Johnson."

The dress Mrs. Patterson ordered was for her sister, who was expected to arrive in Washington three weeks later. Both of President Johnson's daughters wore the same size and liked long sleeves and high necklines with collars. The Johnson sisters were pleased with Lizzie's work and became regular customers.

When Lizzie visited the White House to fit their dresses, she found that the White House had changed considerably. Crews of workmen painted and hung new wallpaper. Linen slipcovers hid stained and damaged upholstery. Congress appropriated seventy-six thousand dollars to restore and repair the White House.

Lizzie knew in her heart she no longer wanted to visit the executive mansion or work for the current first family. The Johnsons were no friends of Mrs. Lincoln. President Johnson sent no condolence message to Mrs.

Lincoln after her husband's assassination or even inquired after her health. Lizzie took such slights to Mrs. Lincoln personally. Besides, he certainly was no friend to the Negro people. He vetoed the first Civil Rights Act of 1866, which declared Negroes were citizens of the United States and entitled to equal treatment under the law.

When one of the sisters wrote Lizzie a note requesting that she come to the White House to cut and fit dresses, Lizzie answered with a curt note stating that she never cut material outside her workrooms. In the past, however, when Mrs. Lincoln had insisted upon coming to Lizzie's rooms, Lizzie had remarked, "I never approved of ladies attached to the Presidential household coming to my rooms. I always thought . . . it would be more consistent with their dignity to send for me, and let me come to them, instead of their coming to me." Lizzie's refusal to come to the White House ended her relationship with the Johnson family.

Months passed, and although Lizzie's business prospered, Mrs. Lincoln's absence left a large void in her life. Lizzie devoted more time to sewing in quilting bees and to other charitable works in the black Presbyterian church she attended a few blocks from her boardinghouse. In the church's basement a school was organized with four black students, and it eventually became the first public black high school in the United States. Her association with the Lincolns set her apart from the other congregants. Some felt uncomfortable in her presence. When she walked down the aisle to her pew on Sundays, people turned to look at her. What they saw was a tall distinguished woman, exquisitely dressed, who exuded great charm and social grace. Sometimes she would hear whispers behind her back and the name Mrs. Lincoln. Mrs. Lincoln wrote letters to Lizzie almost every day, sometimes twice a day. Old and new debts borrowed at a high interest rate made the former first lady more desperate than usual. Her letters reflected her hopelessness. A growing uneasiness filled Lizzie with each of Mrs. Lincoln's letters.

CHAPTER FOURTEEN

IN THE FALL of 1865 Betty Garland Longstreet, wife of Confederate general James Longstreet and cousin of Lizzie's former master, Hugh Garland, visited Lizzie's rooms. As a girl, Mrs. Longstreet often visited the Garlands when Lizzie lived with them in Dinwiddie township. Lizzie was delighted to see her. She had lost track of her former slaveowners during the war but had often wondered about them.

Now Mrs. Longstreet informed Lizzie that the family had returned from Vicksburg, Mississippi, to Virginia. Nannie, the Garland daughter who as a baby had slept in Lizzie's bed until Lizzie left the family, had married a Confederate general from one of the most prominent families in Virginia. They now lived on an estate in the Shenandoah Valley.

Lizzie said, "I can't believe it; she was just a child when I last saw her. And so my little pet is married."

Mrs. Longstreet also brought sad news. Fannie, another of the daughters Lizzie had cared for, had died of dysentery soon after her sisters, Mary and Carrie, had died five years earlier in Lizzie's arms. Hugh, Jr., the older of the two Garland boys, had been killed as a Confederate soldier the year before.

Of the seven Garland children, only three lived— Spott, Maggie, and Nannie—and each wanted to see Lizzie. So did their mother, Mrs. Garland, Lizzie's former mistress.

Lizzie exclaimed, "I should be delighted to go to them."

When Lizzie had expressed interest in the Garlands' welfare during the war, her Northern friends would roll their eyes in surprise. "Why, Lizzie," they would say, "how can you have a kind thought for those who inflicted a terrible wrong upon you by keeping you in bondage?"

Lizzie would answer, "The past is a mirror that re-

Confederate Colonel Hugh A. Garland, Jr., killed November 30, 1864. (BY PERMISSION OF THE MISSOURI HISTORICAL SOCIETY.)

flects the chief incidents of my life. To surrender it is to surrender the greatest part of my existence—early impressions, friends and the graves of my father, my mother and my son."

After Mrs. Longstreet left, Lizzie immediately wrote to Nannie Garland, who replied promptly, "You must come to me, dear Lizzie. I am dying to see you. Ma, Maggie, Spott and Minnie, sister Mary's child, are with me, and only you are needed to make the circle complete. Come; I will not take no for an answer."

Lizzie arranged her work schedule so she could be away for a few weeks in August. On August 10, 1865, the anniversary of her son's death four years earlier, Lizzie left Washington for Harpers Ferry, the town where John Brown had led his raid to free slaves in 1859. The townspeople now honored him as a hero. Photos and souvenirs of him were sold in almost every store.

Lizzie boarded the train designated for black people. Jim Crow laws, which segregated white and black people in restaurants, transport vehicles, and schools, were in force everywhere.

The rhythmic sound of the train wheels lulled Lizzie to sleep. She overslept and didn't get off at the stop where she was supposed to change trains. Now she had to transfer to two other trains. Finally, she boarded the stagecoach for Rude's Hill, where Nannie lived. Once again, she overslept and missed her stop.

The stage dropped her off at four o'clock in the morning at New Market, a small village six miles past Rude's Hill. A trip that should have taken no more than a day had taken two and a half days.

Lizzie entered a run-down hotel that served Negroes, and ordered a cup of coffee. When she recounted her roundabout trip to the clerk behind the counter, an elderly black man seated in the corner of the room offered to drive her to Rude's Hill in his wagon.

As the wagon approached Rude's Hill, Lizzie saw a young man, Spott Garland, standing before a grand house set in an expansive yard and shaded with locust trees. He ran down a long path, yelling, "Lizzie is here! Lizzie is here!"

Within a moment the doorway was crammed with people, each trying to get out at once.

In her eagerness to reach them, Lizzie stepped onto the wagon's stile intending to leap into the yard. Momentarily she forgot that, at forty-eight, she was no longer the nimble girl of her youth. Now, her hoop skirt caught on the wagon's post, and she fell headlong into the yard, her face buried in dry dirt.

Spott lifted her and placed her into the outstretched arms of his sisters, Nannie and Maggie, and their mother. It had been more than five years since Lizzie had seen them.

Minnie, the young daughter of deceased Mary Garland, joined the excitement of her uncle, aunts, and grandmother. She had heard much about Lizzie.

They carried Lizzie into the parlor, where they placed her in an easy chair before a bright morning fire. The morning was unseasonably brisk for August.

Spott carried her belongings to the guest bedroom while servants from different parts of the house came to witness the scene in utter amazement.

"You look as young as when you left us in St. Louis, years ago," they said as they hovered over Lizzie. Nannie hugged and kissed her over and over again.

Mrs. Garland asked Lizzie if she had had breakfast, and before she could respond, the other members of the family answered in unison, "No, she has not."

The three Garland children and their niece started for the kitchen at once to prepare Lizzie's breakfast. Mrs. Garland pointed to the Negro cook who stood in the room with the other servants, incredulously watching the Garlands and Lizzie. Mrs. Garland called after her children that it was not necessary for them to make Lizzie's breakfast. They ignored her.

While Lizzie sat resting her feet on a footstool eating breakfast, the cook broke the silence that filled the room. She said she had never seen people carry on so, and wondered aloud whether the family would hug and kiss her, prepare and serve her food, if she should go off and stay away so long.

During her five-week stay at Rude's Hill, Lizzie dined with the Garlands, attended tournaments, and visited their friends. On one of several horseback-riding trips, Nannie's husband laughed and said, "Why, Lizzie, you are riding with Colonel Gilmore [Harry Gilmore, a prominent former Confederate soldier]. Just think of the change from Lincoln to Gilmore!" To him, their riding together meant the racial hatred that had divided the country no longer existed. He predicted brighter days ahead for the North and the South.

During one of Lizzie's long talks with her former slave mistress, Mrs. Garland told her she had thought about her almost every day of the war and longed to see her. When her family learned she was with Mrs. Lincoln, everyone told her she was foolish to think of ever seeing Lizzie again. Mrs. Garland said, "But I knew your heart, and could not believe that you would forget us. I always argued that you would come and see us some day."

Lizzie answered, "You judged me rightly, Miss Ann.

How could I forget you whom I had grown up with from infancy?"

Mrs. Garland faltered as she asked, "Do you always feel kindly towards me, Lizzie?"

Lizzie answered, "I have but one unkind thought, and that is, . . . you did not give me the advantage of a good education. What I have learned has been the study of after years."

Mrs. Garland sadly nodded her head in agreement. She said, "I did not look at things then as I do now. I have always regretted that you were not educated when a girl." With a touch of envy in her voice, she continued, "But you have not suffered much on this score, since you get along in the world better than we who enjoyed every educational advantage in childhood."

When Lizzie looked at things that way, she agreed. However, how could Mrs. Garland understand how much better her life would have been with an education? Lizzie would always feel that void and longing.

Things being the way they were, Lizzie wrote about her five weeks at Rude's Hill, "they were five of the most delightful weeks of my life."

CHAPTER FIFTEEN

LIZZIE PLANNED TO visit Richmond after her stay at Rude's Hill but changed her mind when she heard that a cholera epidemic was raging there. Returning to Washington left her feeling empty, so she decided instead to settle in Baltimore. After remaining there a short time, however, she returned to the nation's capital. Baltimore failed to fill the void in her life that the Lincolns had left.

Lizzie rounded up her former employees and reopened her business. Once again her workrooms were filled with orders for ball gowns and other women's apparel.

At the beginning of January 1866, the Congressional Committee on House Appropriations convened to investigate criminal charges against Mrs. Lincoln. Rumors circulated that she had stripped the executive mansion of beds, bedding, table linen, housekeeping utensils, china, and other items. And that she had sold them. The committee summoned several witnesses to testify about the number of boxes Mrs. Lincoln had been furnished, what they contained, where and how they had been sent, and what bills she had ordered to be paid before she left.

No congressional records show that Lizzie was summoned before the committee, although virtually everyone else who worked in the White House was questioned. Why the committee failed to interview Lizzie, the most knowledgeable of all the witnesses, is uncertain. The committee closed its investigation after finding no criminal evidence against Mrs. Lincoln.

In the spring of 1867, Lizzie received a letter from Maggie Garland requesting permission to visit and stay with Lizzie. Lizzie replied immediately, "Yes, come by all means. I shall be so glad to see you."

The two women stayed up nights, laughing and talking about old times. Maggie told Lizzie that her Southern friends had been scandalized when they heard she planned to lodge in Lizzie's rooms. Even after she explained to them that she loved Lizzie like a second mother, they failed to understand.

Soon after Maggie left, Lizzie received a troubled letter from Mrs. Lincoln: "It will not be startling news to you, my dear Lizzie, to learn that I must sell a portion of my wardrobe to add to my resources, so as to enable me to live decently. . . . I cannot live on $1,700 a year, and as I have many costly things which I shall never wear, I might as well turn them into money. . . . It is humiliating to be placed in such a position, but as I am in the position, I must extricate myself as best I can." She asked Lizzie to meet her in New York to help her sell a portion of her wardrobe.

Although Lizzie would have to close her business, once again she placed Mrs. Lincoln's needs above her own. While several letters passed between them, Lizzie told no one of Mrs. Lincoln's plan.

The two women planned to get together in the middle of September. Mrs. Lincoln instructed Lizzie to meet her in New York, where she would rent rooms for them at a second-class hotel under the assumed name of Mrs. Clarke.

Lizzie felt uneasy. Under an assumed name, Mrs. Lincoln would not be accorded the respect the Lincoln name commanded. And residing in a second-rate hotel would make her feel more sorry for herself than ever. And, most critically, no hotel proprietor would rent rooms to Lizzie, a black woman.

When Lizzie arrived at the St. Denis Hotel, she rang the bell at the ladies' entrance, handed her calling card to the young man who answered the door, and asked him to take it to "Mrs. Clarke."

Mrs. Lincoln, seated in the parlor of the hotel writing letters, heard Lizzie's voice and promptly came into the hall. She hugged Lizzie and exclaimed how glad she was to see her. Mrs. Lincoln then tried to rent a room for Lizzie adjoining her own. Without looking at either woman, the hotel clerk answered, "We have no room for her, madam."

Mrs. Lincoln replied, "But she must have a room. She is a friend of mine, and I want a room for her adjoining mine."

The clerk snarled, "Friend of yours or not, I tell you we have no room for her on your floor. I can find a place for her on the fifth floor."

Lizzie was mortified. Not for herself, but for Mrs. Lincoln. As a black woman, Lizzie was accustomed to being treated as a second-class citizen when she was away from the Lincolns. But no clerk ever dared treat Mrs. Lincoln in such an undignified manner. Of course, he had no idea who she was.

Before Lizzie could say anything, Mrs. Lincoln retorted, "That, sir, I presume, will be a vast improvement on my room . . . if she goes to the fifth floor, I shall go too, sir. What is good enough for her is good enough for me."

The two middle-aged women climbed five flights of steep stairs. Lizzie wrote, "I thought we should never reach the top; and when we did . . . what accommodations! Three-cornered tiny rooms scantily furnished. I never expected to see the widow of President Lincoln in such dingy, humble quarters."

Mrs. Lincoln sat down heavily, breathless from the climb, and said, "I will give them [the hotel management] a regular going over in the morning."

The next morning Lizzie tried to persuade Mrs. Lincoln to register under her own name at another hotel. Although she agreed to move, she wouldn't reveal her identity. In the new hotel, however, they were able to settle into adjoining rooms.

Mrs. Lincoln had hired the firm of Brady & Company to sell her jewelry. W. H. Brady and S. C. Keyes, the firm's representatives, arrived at the hotel soon after the women were settled. They persuaded Mrs. Lincoln to give them not only her jewelry to sell but her other personal possessions as well. They promised to raise at least one hundred thousand dollars in a few weeks, predicting that people everywhere would help her when they learned of her poverty. Lizzie worried about the powerful influence the diamond brokers exercised over the former first lady. There was something about the men that made Lizzie distrust them.

Because the brokers dealt mostly with jewelry, Lizzie reasoned that she and Mrs. Lincoln would fare better selling her apparel directly to secondhand clothing dealers. Lizzie visited several merchants and arranged for each to call on Mrs. Lincoln at their hotel. When the dealers arrived and examined the garments, however, not knowing they belonged to Mrs. Lincoln, they found the prices too high.

Within the same week, carrying bundles of worn dresses and shawls over their arms, Lizzie and Mrs. Lincoln drove in a horse-drawn, enclosed, darkened carriage and visited other secondhand shops. The clothing dealers offered very little for the used garments. Mrs. Lincoln, however, accepted their terms for a few of her things. Both women returned to the hotel tired and disgusted.

The diamond brokers persuaded Mrs. Lincoln to write letters exposing her impoverished condition. They planned to show the letters to prominent politicians and threaten to publish them in major newspapers throughout the country if they failed to either donate or vote funds to help her. The brokers predicted that politicians would make big donations rather than have the letters published for the nation to read.

Lizzie stood at Mrs. Lincoln's elbow while she wrote the letters and implored her to use the mildest language possible so they did not appear threatening. Lizzie knew politicians would respond unfavorably to threats.

Mrs. Lincoln ignored her warning. She said, "Never mind, Lizzie, anything to raise the wind. One might as well be killed for a sheep as a lamb."

The letters failed to persuade politicians to donate money and served only to make them angry and condemn Mrs. Lincoln as a "national embarrassment." Mrs. Lincoln's visit to New York proved to be a disaster.

Refusing to admit defeat, she encouraged the brokers to display her wardrobe for sale in their showrooms. She gave them permission to have her letters published in a widely circulated newspaper, the *World*.

Lizzie accompanied Mrs. Lincoln to the station, where the former first lady boarded a train for Chicago. Although Lizzie desperately wanted to return to Washington, Mrs. Lincoln implored her to stay in New York and watch over her jewelry and clothing.

Mrs. Lincoln wrote to her as soon as she arrived in Chicago:

> My dear Lizzie, do visit Mr. Brady [W. H. Brady, one of the diamond brokers] each morning at 9 o'clock and nudge them all you can. . . . How much I miss you, tongue cannot tell. . . . I consider you my best living friend, and I am struggling to be enabled some day to repay you. Write me often, as you promised.
>
> Always truly yours,
> M.L.

The day after Mrs. Lincoln's letters were published in the *World*, Mrs. Lincoln wrote a frantic letter to Lizzie:

> My dear Lizzie; I am writing this morning with a broken heart after a sleepless night of great mental suffering. R [Mrs. Lincoln's eldest son, Robert] came up last evening like a maniac, and almost threatening [to take] his life, looking like death, because the letters of *The World* were published in yesterday's paper. I could not refrain from weeping when I saw him so miserable. But yet, my dear good Lizzie, was it not to protect myself and help others—and was not my motive and action of the purest kind? Pray for me that this cup of affliction may pass from me, or

be sanctified to me. I weep whilst I am writing. I pray for death this morning. Only my darling Taddie prevents my taking my life. I shall have to endure a round of newspaper abuse . . . because I dared venture to relieve a few of my wants. Tell Mr. Brady and Keyes not to have a line of mine once more in print. I am nearly losing my reason.   Your friend,

M. L.

Mrs. Lincoln's clothing remained on display, but little of it sold. The men decided to sell the wardrobe at a public auction where rooms of clothes overflowed with hundreds of curious onlookers who came to view the widow's wardrobe. Twenty-five dresses, folded or tossed about by frequent handling, lay on a piano and a chaise lounge. Shawls hung over backs of chairs.

Every newspaper in the land carried the story of Mrs. Lincoln's wardrobe sale. An article in the *New York Evening Express* stated that "the majority of the visitors is adverse to the course Mrs. Lincoln has thought to pursue, and the criticisms are severe . . . prices range from $25 to $75. Some of them, if not worn long, have been worn much; they are jagged under the arms and at the bottom of the skirt, stains are on the lining and other objections present themselves to those who oscillate between the dresses and dollars. . . . Other dresses . . . have scarcely been worn—one, perhaps, while Mrs. Lincoln sat for her picture and from one the basting threads had not yet been removed. . . . The peculiarity of the dresses is that . . . most of them are low necked—a taste which some ladies attribute to Mrs. Lincoln's appreciation of her own bust."

Mrs. Lincoln's wardrobe is examined by curious spectators in 1866. (USED BY
PERMISSION OF THE LLOYD OSTENDORF COLLECTION, DAYTON, OHIO.)

Newspapers everywhere condemned Mrs. Lincoln.
One of the *Illinois Springfield Journal* editorials stated
that Mrs. Lincoln had been known to be deranged for
years and should be pitied for all her strange acts.

In one of many letters Mrs. Lincoln wrote to Lizzie,
she commented on her treatment by American journal-
ists: "These low creatures are allowed to hurl their mali-
cious wrath at me, with no one to defend me or protect
me if I starve. Their aim is to prevent my goods being
sold, or anything being done for me."

Lizzie could no longer sit idly by while the press
abused her friend because it failed to understand her.

CHAPTER SIXTEEN

IN AN EFFORT to defend Mrs. Lincoln from the vicious attacks of the press, Lizzie visited the editor of the *New York Evening News* and reminded him that the empress of France frequently disposed of her used clothing publicly without being subjected to unkind criticism. She pointed out that many famous foreigners frequently visited stores under assumed names to avoid being recognized. She explained that Mrs. Lincoln had put her wardrobe up for sale as a desperate move. Lizzie showed him a letter Mrs. Lincoln had sent to her in which she wrote, "Elizabeth, if evil comes from this, pray for my deliverance, as I did it for the best."

On October 12, 1867, the editor printed the information Lizzie furnished him, including parts of Mrs. Lincoln's letters to Lizzie. His article began, "Mrs. Lincoln feels sorely aggrieved at many of the harsh criticisms that have been passed upon her for traveling incognito . . . she adopted this course . . . desiring to avoid publicity. Hundreds passed her who had courted her good graces when she reigned supreme at the White House."

Lizzie wrote to Frederick Douglass, now editor of the *North Star* newspaper, about helping Mrs. Lincoln. He wrote back on October 18: "My Dear Mrs. Keckley: You judge me rightly—I am willing to do what I can to place the widow of our martyred President in the affluent position which her relation to that good man and to the

Frederick Douglass, frontispiece in My Bondage & My Freedom. (BY PERMISSION OF MOORLAND-SPINGARN RESEARCH CENTER, HOWARD UNIVERSITY.)

country entitles her to. . . . The best speakers in the country should be secured for that purpose."

Around the end of September or the beginning of October Lizzie contacted the Reverend Henry Highland Garnet, a personal friend of the Lincolns, who led one of the largest black congregations in New York. He, too, offered to lecture on Mrs. Lincoln's behalf.

In October of 1867 Lizzie addressed black congregations all over New York, who agreed to collect money to relieve Mrs. Lincoln's distress. She said, "The colored people recognize Abraham Lincoln as their great friend, and they were anxious to show their kind interest in the welfare of his family in some way more earnest and sustantial than simple words."

When Lizzie informed Mrs. Lincoln of the black community's plan to help her, she received a curt reply: "I fear you are only losing your time in N.Y. and that I shall be left in debt for what I am owing the firm [Brady & Company] . . . I want neither Mr. Douglass nor Garnet to lecture in my behalf. The conduct in N.Y. is disgusting me with the whole business."

In November of 1867 when Lizzie showed Mrs. Lincoln's letter to Mr. Douglass and the Reverend Garnet, they immediately abandoned their plans. The black congregations canceled their collections.

Weeks later Mrs. Lincoln reconsidered. As an incentive to renew Lizzie's efforts, she offered to pay Lizzie $300 per year and to return the collected money to the black community upon her death. Her initial curt refusal, however, had stifled the black community's enthusiasm.

Lizzie planned to conduct a European exhibit of the Lincoln mementos Mrs. Lincoln had given her, including the bloodstained cape the former first lady wore the night of her husband's assassination. Lizzie would donate the proceeds of the exhibit to help Mrs. Lincoln's financial plight. In January of 1868 when she informed Mrs. Lincoln of her project, the former first lady was horrified by the idea. "Your letter announcing that my clothes were to be paraded in Europe—those I gave you—has almost turned me wild," she wrote back on January 12, 1868. "For the sake of *humanity* if not for *me* and my children, *do not* have these black clothes displayed in Europe. The thought has almost whitened every hair on my head."

Lizzie immediately abandoned the idea.

Lizzie was not one to write many letters to Mrs. Lincoln, but she continued to receive letter after letter from the troubled widow, who described herself as "so nervous and miserable." She asked Lizzie to remain in New York a little longer to oversee her affairs. And she warned that newspaper stories would soon appear stating President Lincoln had left her well provided for. Mrs. Lincoln convinced Lizzie the figures looked better on paper than in real life. She wanted Lizzie to explain to everyone in New York that no matter what they read, she was poor.

Mrs. Lincoln's feelings for Lizzie are apparent from her letters. For example: "I had hoped, if something was gained [from the sale of her jewelry and clothing], to have immediately placed you in more pleasant circumstances. Write me, do, when you receive this. Your silence pains me." And another: "How hard it is that I cannot see and talk with you in this time of great great trouble. I feel as if I had not a friend in the world save yourself."

Mrs. Lincoln fretted about her clothes for sale at Brady & Company and wanted Lizzie to return them to her: "I fear my articles (. . .) are getting pulled to pieces and soiled. I do not wish you to leave N.Y. without having the finest articles packed and returned to me."

Mrs. Lincoln included a list of these items. The total value of Mrs. Lincoln's wardrobe that she had offered for sale was twenty-five thousand dollars.

In the quiet of a room Lizzie rented in a boardinghouse, she collected her thoughts. Most steps she had taken to help Mrs. Lincoln had been thwarted, and the newspapers continued to hurl abuse. Lizzie was more convinced than ever that if people knew Mrs. Lincoln as she did, they would not only understand but forgive her actions.

Lizzie decided to set the record straight once and for all. Over the years, many people had often told her she should write a book, because her own life was fascinating and her relationship with Mrs. Lincoln placed her in a special light. Lizzie was well acquainted with the power of the printed word.

Thousands of former slaves were telling their stories with the help of professional writers. Lizzie would tell her own story and that of Mrs. Lincoln with the help of a professional writer. The book she proposed to write would tell of the good and bad aspects of her own meager background and set the record straight for Mrs. Lincoln by exposing her strengths and weaknesses. Lizzie planned to share profits of the book with Mrs. Lincoln. Exactly how Lizzie and the New York publisher Carleton & Company came together is not clear. James Redpath, a well-known writer and editor who ran a speakers' bureau, was chosen to help her record her story. She may have known him from St. Louis, where, as a staunch abolitionist, he had traveled about the city interviewing slaves. Or she may have met him at the White House, where he was a frequent visitor, advising President Lincoln to recognize the independence of Haiti. Redpath came to Lizzie's room each afternoon or evening and took notes while she talked to him for several hours. After writing up his notes, he would return the next day, read what he had written, and then take down more for the following day.

Lizzie moved to a fourth-floor garret in another house and took in sewing to support herself while she spent long hours thinking and remembering. Often the memories brought pain, but they failed to stop her. Mostly at night, she jotted down recollections of events she planned to tell Redpath about the next day.

Lizzie shared with Redpath her grave concern about embarrassing Mrs. Lincoln by divulging her personal thoughts and confidential dealings for the world to read. Redpath promised that nothing published in the book would hurt Mrs. Lincoln. Lizzie gave him twenty-three personal letters Mrs. Lincoln had sent to her. She was fully aware of the importance of personal correspondence to the authenticity of a biography from her days with the Garlands when Mr. Garland was writing about the life of John Randolph. Redpath promised not to publish anything from Mrs. Lincoln's letters that would embarrass the former first lady.

Some historians believe Mrs. Lincoln knew of Lizzie's plan to write the book; others think she did not. Aside from the time Lizzie arranged for the Negro community to help Mrs. Lincoln financially, Lizzie rarely took action on anything that concerned Mrs. Lincoln without her prior knowledge and approval.

The title of Lizzie's book was *Behind the Scenes or Thirty Years a Slave and Four Years in the White House*. In the preface she wrote: "It may be charged that I have written too freely . . . especially in regard to Mrs. Lincoln. I do

Elizabeth Hobbs Keckley. This photo was taken in the 1890s while Lizzie taught at Wilberforce University. Lizzie gave the photo to Dr. William Board while he was a student at the institution. (COURTESY OF THE LINCOLN MUSEUM, FORT WAYNE, INDIANA, A PART OF THE LINCOLN NATIONAL CORPORATION.)

not think so; at least I have been prompted by the purest motives. . . . The people have judged her harshly, and no woman was ever more traduced in the public prints of the country. . . . The people knew nothing of the secret history of her transactions. . . . If I have betrayed confidence in anything I have published, it has been to place Mrs. Lincoln in a better light before the world. . . . My own character, as well as the character of Mrs. Lincoln, is at stake, since I have been intimately associated with that lady in the most eventful periods of her life. I have been her confidante, and if evil charges are laid at her door, they also must be laid at mine, since I have been a party to all her movements."

It is not clear why the title of Lizzie Keckley's book claims she served as a slave for thirty years when, according to the date on her slave papers and on those she filled out for a pension, she had been a slave for thirty-seven years. Perhaps Redpath recorded the information incorrectly, or the publishing company decided to shorten the length of the title. Or perhaps Lizzie preferred her patrons and readers to think of her as a younger woman. Whatever the reasons, many articles about Lizzie state she was born in 1825 because of this mistake.

CHAPTER SEVENTEEN

THE AMERICAN LITERARY Gazette & Publisher's Circular of April 1, 1868, contained the following notice:

G. W. Carlton [sic] and Co.
Will publish early in April A Remarkable Book
entitled Behind the Scenes

By Mrs. Elizabeth Keckley 30 years a slave in the best Southern families. . . . She discloses the whole history of Mrs. Lincoln's unfortunate attempts to dispose of her wardrobe, etc, which when read will remove many erroneous impressions in the public mind, and place Mrs. Lincoln in a more favorable light.

One Vol. 12 mo. 400 pp. cloth. Illustrated with portrait of the author. Price $2.00

Through some misunderstanding, oversight, or purposeful action, every one of Mrs. Lincoln's unedited letters to Lizzie was published at the back of the book. The book provided new fodder for both the press and the public to condemn Mrs. Lincoln and Lizzie as well. Lizzie had dared to write a biography of Mary Todd Lincoln and reveal personal information. Many of those mentioned in her book were alive and indignant. Forces determined to suppress information and stop black women from speaking out made Lizzie an example of what would happen to those who did. Critics wrote vicious reviews of her book. Some said that Lizzie was too ignorant and uneducated to have written it. Others called it "backstairs gossip" and said its disclosures desecrated the memory of President Lincoln. Many of her friends, both white and black, turned against Lizzie. White people believed she had betrayed Mrs. Lincoln. Black people feared that white employers would never trust Negro help again. Robert Lincoln was so furious over the book's disclosure of private information and intimate details of his parents' relationship that he prevailed upon the publisher, Carleton & Company, to recall it from the market. He persuaded his friends to buy and burn all remaining copies. Lizzie tried to explain her motives for writing the book and to apologize for any pain she had inadvertently caused, but Robert Lincoln refused to see her. *Behind the Scenes or Thirty Years a Slave and Four Years in the White House* was never widely circulated in Lizzie's lifetime, and she earned no profit from its publication. Mrs. Lincoln's letters were never returned to her by the publisher.

A writer anonymously published a parody of Lizzie's book, entitled *Behind the Seams* by a Nigger Woman Who Took in Work from Mrs. Lincoln and Mrs. Davis. The author signed it "Betsy Kickley, (Nigger) X Her mark."

With the publication of Lizzie's book, Mrs. Lincoln felt that her last remaining friend had betrayed her. She never saw Lizzie again, although it is reported that some letters were exchanged between them. Lizzie made a quilt for her in the 1870s that presently exists in a collection owned by Ross Trump of Medina, Ohio. His mother purchased it from one of the Lincoln heirs, and it periodically tours the country with other famous quilts.

No letters that Lizzie wrote to Mrs. Lincoln are known to exist. The former first lady usually destroyed personal correspondence, and after her death, Robert Lincoln burned many personal papers belonging to his parents.

Mrs. Lincoln returned briefly to Washington from Chicago a month after the publication of *Behind the Scenes* to attend Robert's wedding. Immediately afterward, she and Tad left the country for an indefinite stay in Europe, where she traveled under an assumed name. It was said that Lizzie's book was the final blow that drove her from the country. Whenever Mrs. Lincoln referred to Lizzie after the publication of her book, she derisively called her the "coloured historian."

Lizzie rarely spoke of the book during the rest of her life, and when she did, it was with pain. The loss of Mrs. Lincoln's friendship left a wound that never completely healed. She moved from the Walker Lewis Boardinghouse in Washington and from house to house in the nation's capital each year for several years. She seemed to find peace nowhere.

When Mrs. Lewis died, Lizzie returned to the boardinghouse to care for Mrs. Lewis's two young daughters. She continued to support herself as a dressmaker and teacher, although her clientele never reached its former heights.

She found solace in regularly attending services in her church, where she volunteered her time and donated money. She paid monthly dues to the Columbian Harmony Society, a black burial association that guaranteed its members a dignified and stately funeral. Dues were used to purchase individual grave sites, engraved marble headstones, and everlasting care.

Lizzie's mother had been buried in an unmarked grave. To Lizzie, this was the final indignity of slavery. And although her son died a free man, he also lay buried in an unmarked site. She would make sure her own grave was marked clearly with a stately, inscribed stone. She set aside money for a monument and four posts and a rail to surround her grave. For her final resting place, she chose a beautiful knoll in Washington's Harmony Cemetery facing east, beneath a large sprawling elm tree.

Mary Lincoln returned from Europe with Tad, arriving in Chicago in May of 1871. Three months after Tad's eighteenth birthday, he died of what physicians termed "compression of the heart."

Perhaps it was the death of her beloved sons and husband, combined with the loss of Lizzie's friendship and an accumulation of everything else that had gone wrong with her life, that pushed Mrs. Lincoln over the edge. Her bizarre behavior now became more extreme. She purchased $600 worth of window curtains, although she had no home to hang them in (she boarded at a hotel in Chicago). She bought seventeen pairs of gloves and spent $1,150 for three watches and other jewelry, although, since her husband's assassination, she had worn no jewelry. She sewed $56,000 worth of government bonds into the pockets of the petticoats she wore to go shopping. Her hotel closets were filled with unopened packages. She heard voices speak to her through the walls and floors of her room. She reported several times that her purse had been stolen, that her son, Robert, tried to kill her, and that Chicago was on fire. She wandered about the hotel in her nightdress and could be seen talking to imaginary people. In 1875 Robert Lincoln hired a detective to trail her and report on her activities.

Driven to desperation by his mother's behavior, Robert had his mother declared insane. His attorney visited Mrs. Lincoln's hotel room and gave her one hour's notice of her trial. She had no time to select her own attorney or to prepare her defense or to groom herself. Two deputies waited in the hotel's lobby carrying warrants that entitled them to use force if she refused to voluntarily come to court accompanied by her son's attorney. Among the many who testified against her besides Robert were the manager of the hotel, maids, store clerks, and doctors who never examined her. A jury of twelve men found her to be insane, a threat to the safety of society, and incompetent to handle her own affairs. Her name was entered onto page 596 of the "Lunatic Record" for Cook County, State of Illinois. The court sentenced her to be confined in a private sanitarium forty miles from Chicago. Within hours of the verdict, Mary Lincoln attempted suicide. After serving less than four months as a patient, Mrs. Lincoln secured her own release with the help of a judge and his wife, the first woman attorney in Illinois.

The former first lady fled to Europe. In 1880, she returned to Springfield, Illinois, and moved into the home of her sister and her sister's husband, Ninian Edwards, where she had married President Lincoln forty years before. She wore a money belt day and night, accused her sister of stealing her things, spent much time rifling through her sixty-four trunks of goods that she had moved to the Edwardses' house, and kept three thousand dollars' worth of gold in a top dresser drawer. She secluded herself in a darkened bedroom and died on July 16, 1882.

In 1888 Mr. Lincoln's friend and former law partner of twenty years, William H. Herndon, an outspoken enemy of Mrs. Lincoln, wrote a controversial biography, *Herndon's Lincoln*, with the help of coauthor Jessie W. Weik. Herndon states in the preface of his book that he attempts to present an honest look at Abraham Lincoln with complimentary as well as uncomplimentary facts. Among other things, the book claims that Lincoln's parents were not married when he was born, that he was not a practicing Christian, that his first and only true love had been Ann Rutledge, that he never loved Mary Lincoln and had been intimidated into marrying her. Over the years Lincoln historians have disproved many of these falsehoods.

Herndon's Lincoln received crushing reviews. One Midwest newspaper called it the "vaporings of a silly old man," another, "a gross and infamous slander from beginning to end" intended "to poison the minds of decent people against the dead President and martyr." Many critics agreed with a Nebraska newspaper that called it "the work of a sneak and a villain." After the book was published, the authors received many complaints that no copies were available to purchase. The authors suspected that Robert Lincoln had suppressed the book, just as he had done with Lizzie's.

Three years after the publication of *Herndon's Lincoln,* on April 2, 1891, Lizzie sent coauthor Jesse Weik two locks of hair, one of President Lincoln's that she had snipped the night after his assassination, and one of Willie's. She also sent along a piece of Mrs. Lincoln's white satin gown with the long ruffled train that led President Lincoln to remark, "Our cat has a long tail tonight," as well as a piece of the gown Mrs. Lincoln wore to the second inauguration. One wonders why Lizzie presented treasured mementos to one who had coauthored a derogatory account of the Lincolns. Perhaps it was because Herndon had died two weeks before and she sent them as a token of condolence, or perhaps because Lizzie truly believed that the authors were sincere and honest in what they reported no matter how the information was condemned. She knew what it felt like to be castigated for honest and sincere motives.

In 1892 Lizzie left Washington for Xenia, Ohio, to teach in the Department of Sewing and Domestic Science Arts at Wilberforce University, the university for black students where her son, George, had been a student more than thirty years before.

Lizzie had a large trunk in which she kept scraps of fabric she had saved from many of Mrs. Lincoln's gowns. She gave small pieces to her favorite pupils so they could make them into pincushions.

Sewing had changed dramatically in the years since

Original buildings of Wilberforce University, 1856. (USED BY PERMISSION OF REMBERT E. STOKES LEARNING RESOURCES CENTER LIBRARY, WILBERFORCE UNIVERSITY.)

Lizzie had her first experiences with a needle. In those days there were almost no ready-to-wear garments available. Now women's clothing could be ordered through catalogs or purchased at stores. Cutting machines cut easily through five thicknesses of cloth.

A year after Lizzie arrived at Wilberforce, the school participated in the 1893 Columbian World's Exposition in Chicago, an event that celebrated the four hundredth anniversary of the discovery of America by Columbus. Lizzie and several of her students traveled to Chicago to represent Wilberforce's exhibit in the Manufacturers and Liberal Arts Building, the largest building ever constructed in the world at that time. The rectangular structure covered thirty-one acres. Its central hall, just one-third of its area, could comfortably seat fifty thousand people.

Fifty nations were represented, and more than twenty-seven million people visited the fair, where the

West and south facades of the Manufacturers and Liberal Arts Building, Columbian World's Exposition, 1893. (USED BY PERMISSION OF THE CHICAGO HISTORICAL SOCIETY.)

Ferris wheel made its first appearance and Cracker Jacks were first served. Buildings costing a total of twenty-five million dollars, housing one hundred million dollars' worth of exhibits, were erected for the occasion.

At the Wilberforce exhibit, Lizzie and her students set up a revolving showcase that displayed photos of all its graduates with a short biography attached to each photo. Prominently visible were wooden figures clothed in creations from Lizzie's dressmaking classes.

In 1898 Lizzie left Wilberforce and returned to Washington. She sewed for as long as her eyes permitted her to see. She retired to the Home for Destitute Women and Children in Washington, D.C. It is thought that funds from the First Black Contraband Relief Association, the organization that she had begun and presided over as president many years before, had been donated

Lizzie's grave in the old Harmony Cemetery. From a photo in They Knew Lincoln *by John E. Washington.*

as a charitable contribution to the home. Lizzie paid monthly dues for room and board at the home from the $12 monthly pension she received as a mother of a dead Civil War soldier.

Lizzie's presence at the home was known only to a few old acquaintances of her church congregation and her pastor. This was the way she wanted it.

Her room was a small one in the basement with one window facing the setting sun. She could look up and out across the street and see black students from Howard

University going to and from classes. Founded in 1867 primarily for black students, the school was one of the first and few universities that conferred advanced academic degrees on men and women of all races. On Lizzie's dresser lay a comb and brush and her Bible. Over it hung a photograph of Mrs. Lincoln. A little table with a pitcher and bowl stood in one corner, a straight chair in another, and a rocking chair in between. An old trunk contained the few clothes she owned.

Lizzie went on carriage rides once a week while at the home and usually wore a long black dress with a soft white triangular scarf about her shoulders tied in the front with a loose knot.

People who knew her at the home said she was always neat, sat rigidly erect at all times, and walked straight as an arrow. Her voice was soft, pleasing, and convincing. She never turned her back while someone spoke, never lingered after good-byes were exchanged, and never permitted anyone to serve her.

Elizabeth Hobbs Keckley died quietly in her sleep on May 26, 1907, at age eighty-eight.

EPILOGUE

ALTHOUGH FEW COPIES of Lizzie's book survived, it remained controversial for more than sixty years. In 1931 the Reverend James H. Stansil of Buffalo, New York, who owned one of the rare copies, republished the book with a partner. In the book's foreword the reverend explains his reasons: "If I were asked what prompted a republication of the book compiled by Elizabeth Keckley, I answer, that after having in my possession for twenty-seven years this book, I thought that the general public might be interested in knowing something of a character who achieved so much in her day and generation. . . . I therefore, commend its pages to the general reader, regardless of race or color; and it is my earnest prayer that it be read in the same spirit in which it has been written; and from a perusal of its pages, it is to be hoped that truth, justice and righteousness will continue to prevail."

The Reverend Stansil's republication of *Behind the Scenes,* however, failed to end the controversy. In 1935 Dr. David Rankin Barbee wrote a newspaper article published in the *Washington Star* stating that there was no such person as Elizabeth Keckley, that a feminist Civil War writer, Jane Swisshelm, wrote *Behind the Scenes.* Barbee's article was quoted by the Associated Press and reprinted in several newspapers throughout the country.

When Dr. John E. Washington, a black dentist and

high school art teacher in Washington, D.C., read the article, he felt compelled to set the record straight. In a letter he wrote to the *Star*, he stated that he knew several seamstresses trained by Elizabeth Keckley and scores of other people who had known her and could testify that she had been Mrs. Lincoln's dressmaker, best friend, and author of *Behind the Scenes*. He photographed her grave site with its headstone and iron posts in the old Harmony Cemetery.

After his letter was printed, Dr. Washington decided to end all doubts about Lizzie once and for all. He wrote a book entitled *They Knew Lincoln*, for which he interviewed more than twenty-five people who knew Lizzie, including the Reverend Francis J. Grimke, whose church she had attended for more than twenty-five years, and who had delivered the eulogy at her funeral.

Dr. Washington asked each person to write him a letter, explain their relationship with Lizzie, and sign it. He published his interviews with them and their letters in his book, which appeared in 1942. In the foreword he wrote, "I believe I would have remained merely a collector of Lincolniana and this book would never have been written but for a bombshell in the form of an article sent to the newspapers by a National Press Service, stating that Mrs. Keckley was not the author of *Behind the Scenes*."

Since the Reverend Stansil's republication of Lizzie's book and the publication of Dr. Washington's book, three different publishing companies have republished *Behind the Scenes*. Lizzie's book is considered an authentic account of the Lincolns' family life during the Civil

War. It is freely quoted by noted historians and used as a text by college professors.

Although Lizzie's purpose for writing the book failed to clear Mary Todd Lincoln's name and aid her financially, her work has brought hidden facts to light and has helped people to better understand Mrs. Lincoln. The ongoing controversy over the former first lady will probably never end. In the past twenty-five years many historians have written authoritative but conflicting accounts of her. Many claim uncomplimentary portraits of her are based on false evidence and skewed by bias; others believe she was not only severely neurotic but truly mean. Scholars often refer to *Behind the Scenes* in their continuing quest to understand Mrs. Lincoln.

New accusations continue to surface. In the spring of 1994 trustees of the Illinois Historical Library released previously hidden segments of former U.S. Senator Orville Hickman Browning's diary. Browning's niece, who sold her uncle's diaries to the state of Illinois eighty years ago, threatened to burn the diaries if bad parts about Mary Lincoln were not blacked out. In 1994 the trustees of the state library decided hiding the information violated the library's role as an archive.

Unfortunately, Lizzie's dream to have her grave site clearly marked and cared for ended in 1960. The cemetery had become overrun with weeds, and its owners ran out of money. A developer who planned to build multiple structures on the land purchased controlling interest in the graveyard and promised to move all the grave sites to a new cemetery in Landover, Maryland. When I went to Landover Cemetery to visit Lizzie's grave in

1989, I was told there was no grave site to visit because Lizzie's remains had been placed in an unmarked grave, her gravestone disposed of since no one had claimed it when gravestones from the old Harmony Cemetery were advertisted in Washington newspapers. The new grave sites in Landover are marked with flat bronze plaques. An administrator at Landover Cemetery claims to have located Lizzie's grave site and says that her remains lie in Lot 115, Grave 7, although no bronze plate marks the site. When asked what happened to unclaimed gravestones from Harmony Cemetery, the same administrator claims they were buried with the remains.

Lizzie's memory and contributions live. The Black Fashion Museum in Harlem, New York, founded in 1979, held an exhibit in 1988 and issued a catalog about Lizzie's life and her achievements. A copy of the gown Lizzie made for Mrs. Lincoln to wear to one of the events of her husband's second inauguration hangs on display there. The original of that gown and another believed to be made by Lizzie for Mrs. Lincoln hang in the First Ladies' Exhibit in the American History Museum of the Smithsonian Institution. Lizzie's name shines brightly in current-day biographies on black women of achievement. . . . including the pages just read.

Lizzie's story of a woman's singular determination to be free and to help and support an emotionally torn first lady continues to live in her book, which is now freely and widely circulated.

BIBLIOGRAPHY

Baker, Jean H. *Mary Todd Lincoln*. New York: Norton, 1987.

Benberry, Cuesta. *Always There: African-American Presence in American Quilts*. The Kentucky Quilt Project, Inc., 1992.

Blassingame, John W. *The Slave Community*. Revised and enlarged edition. New York: Oxford University Press, 1979.

Carpenter, Frank G. *Carp's Washington*. New York: McGraw-Hill, 1960.

Coatsworth, Stella S. *The Loyal People of the Northwest*. Chicago: Church, Goodman & Donnelly Printers, 1869.

Records of the Columbia Historical Society of Washington, D.C. vols. 51 and 52. Edited by J. Kirkpatrick Flack. Charlottesville: The University Press of Virginia, 1984.

Franklin, John Hope. *From Slavery to Freedom*. New York: Random House, 1966.

French, Benjamin Brown. *Witness to the Young Republic, a Yankee's Journal, 1828–1870*. Edited by Donald B. Cole and John J. McDonough. Hanover: University Press of New England, 1989.

Gernon, Blaine Brooks. *The Lincolns in Chicago*. Chicago: Ancarthe Publishers, 1934.

James, Jeannie H., and Wayne C. Temple "Mrs. Lincoln's Clothing." *Lincoln Herald* vol. 62, no. 2 (1960) pp. 54–65.

Jones, Richard L. *Dinwiddie County*. Board of Supervisors of Dinwiddie County, Virginia, 1976.

Keckley, Elizabeth Hobbs. *Behind the Scenes or Thirty Years a Slave and Four Years in the White House*. New York: Arno Press and the New York Times, 1968.

Kunhardt, Dorothy Meserve and Philip B. Kundhardt, Jr. *Twenty Days*. North Hollywood: Newcastle Publishing Co., Inc., 1985.

Leech, Margaret. *Reveille in Washington, 1860–1865*. New York: Harper & Brothers, 1941.

Meem, John Gaw, Jr. *John Gaw Meem and His Decendents*. Charlottesville, Va.: J. L. Meem, 1985.

Neely, Mark E., Jr., & Gerald R. McMurty. *The Insanity File*. Carbondale: Southern Illinois Press, 1986.

Pfanz, Donald C. *Abraham Lincoln at City Point*. Lynchburg, Va.: H. E. Howard, 1989.

Poore, Ben Perley. *Perley's Reminiscences of Sixty Years in the National Metropolis*. Vol. 11. Philadelphia: Hubbard Brothers, 1886.

Quarles, Benjamin. *Negro in the Civil War*. New York: Da Capo Press, 1989.

Randall, Ruth Painter. *Lincoln's Sons*. Boston: Little, Brown and Company, Inc. 1956.

Ross, Ishabel. *Crusades and Crinolines*. New York: Harper & Row, 1963.
———. *The President's Wife*. New York: Putnam, 1973.

Sandburg, Carl. *Abraham Lincoln, the War Years*. Vols. 1–4. New York: Harcourt, Brace, 1939.
———. *Mary Lincoln, Wife and Widow*. New York: Harcourt, Brace, 1932.

Sarten, Jeffrey S. "Infectious Diseases During the Civil War: The Triumph of the Third Army" *Clinical Infectious Diseases*, 16:580–4, University of Chicago, 1993.

Schreiner, Samuel A., Jr. *The Trials of Mrs. Lincoln*. New York: Donald I. Fine, 1987.

Seale, William. *The President's House*. Washington, D.C.: White House Historical Association, 1986.

Smith D. Fry. "Lincoln Liked Her." *Minneapolis Register*, July 6, 1901.

We Are Your Sisters. Edited by Dorothy Sterling. New York: Norton, 1984.

Truman, Major Ben C. *History of the World's Fair*. Chicago: Star Publishing, 1983.

Turner, Justin G. and Linda Levitt Turner. *Mary Todd Lincoln, Her Life and Letters*. New York: Knopf, 1972.

Washington, Dr. John E. *They Knew Lincoln*. New York: Dutton, 1942.

FURTHER SUGGESTED READING

Brent, Linda. *Incidents in the Life of a Slave Girl*. Harvest Books, 1973.

Brown, William Wells. *The Travels of William Wells Brown*. Edited by Paul Jefferson. Markus Wiener Publishers, Inc., 1991.

Burchard, Peter. *Charlotte Forten: A Black Teacher in the Civil War*. Crown, 1995.

Fritz, Jean. *Harriet Beecher Stowe and the Beecher Preachers*. Putnam, 1994.

Hakim, Joy. *A History of the United States: War, Terrible War* (Vol. 6), Oxford, 1994.

Hakim, Joy. *A History of the United States: Reconstruction and Reform* (Vol. 7), Oxford, 1994.

Hamilton, Virginia. *Anthony Burns: The Defeat and Triumph of a Fugitive Slave*. Knopf, 1988.

Hamilton, Virginia. *Many Thousand Gone: African Americans from Slavery to Freedom*. Knopf, 1993.

Lyons, Mary E. *Letters from a Slave Girl: The Story of Harriet Jacobs*. Macmillan, 1992.

McClard, Megan. *Harriet Tubman: Slavery and the Underground Railroad*. Silver Burdett, 1991.

McKissack, Patricia C. and Frederick McKissack. *Sojourner Truth: Ain't I A Woman?* Scholastic, Inc., 1992.

Meltzer, Milton, editor. *A Lincoln in His Own Words*. Harcourt Brace and Company, 1993.

Mettger, Zak. *Till Victory Is Won: Black Soldiers in the Civil War*. Dutton, 1994.

Murphy, Jim. *The Boys War: Confederate and Union Soldiers Talk about the Civil War*. Clarion Books, 1990.

Quarles, Benjamin, editor. *Narrative of the Life of Frederick Douglass, an American Slave, Written by Himself*. The Belknap Press of Harvard University Press, 1960.

Scott, John Anthony and Robert Alan Scott. *John Brown of Harpers Ferry*. Facts on File, 1988.

Taylor, Susie King. *A Black Woman's Civil War Memoirs*. Edited by Patricia W. Romero and Willie Lee Rose. Wiener Publishers, Inc., 1988.

INDEX

In this index, EHK is used for Elizabeth Hobbs Keckley and MTL is used for Mary Todd Lincoln.

Randolph, John, 20, 141
Redpath, James, 140–41, 143
Republican Party, 55
Rheingold, Mrs., 37, 39
Richmond, fall of, 97, 99–100
Runaway slaves, 14, 25–26, 30
Rutledge, Ann, 149

St. Louis, 20, 21, 23, 24, 36
    cholera epidemic, 27, 28
Sanitary Commissions, 116
Schools, illegal, 24–25
Scott, Dred, 28–29
Seward, William H., 107
Sewing circles/classes, 37, 73, 78
Sherman, William Tecumseh, 89
Slave rebellion, 13
Slave trade, 23
Slavery/slaves, 12, 13–14, 68
    children of, 7–8, 14, 23
    EHK, 1, 5, 6–18, 116, 123
    freed, 69–75
    names of, 32 box
    and new territories, 30, 44, 54
    sex forced on women, 18, 32 box
    sold, 7–8
Smithsonian Institution, 158
Springfield, Ill., 51–52, 54, 66

Stansil, James H., 155, 156
Stanton, Edwin M., 104
States and slavery, 26, 30, 54
Stoddard, William O., 83–84
Stowe, Harriet Beecher, 30
Stuart, John Todd, 51
Swisshelm, Jane, 155

They Knew Lincoln (Washington), 156
Truth, Sojourner, 81
Turner, Nat, 13

Uncle Tom's Cabin (Stowe), 30
Underground Railroad, 25

Washington, D.C., 3–4, 53
    and Civil War, 57–60
Washington, John E., 155–56
Weik, Jessie W., 149, 150
Welles, Mary Jane, 108, 109
White House, 63, 112, 119
    receptions at, 46–47, 50, 64, 65, 76, 85, 91, 105–6
Whitman, Walt, 90
Wilberforce University, 25, 39, 54, 76
    EHK teaching at, 150–52